CODING

FOR **PARENTS**

STERLING
New York

An Imprint of Sterling Publishing Co., Inc.
1166 Avenue of the Americas
New York, NY 10036

ISBN: 978-1-4549-2567-5

Distributed in Canada by Sterling Publishing Co., Inc.
c/o Canadian Manda Group, 664 Annette Street
Toronto, Ontario, Canada M6S 2C8

For information about custom editions, special sales, and
premium and corporate purchases, please contact
Sterling Special Sales at 800-805-5489
or specialsales@sterlingpublishing.com

Manufactured in China

2 4 6 8 10 9 7 5 3 1

www.sterlingpublishing.com

CODING

FOR **PARENTS**

FRAZER WILSON

STERLING
New York

FOREWORD

Approaching coding as a learner and also as a guide for kids can be intimidating, but this book will make it easier!

As moms and dads, we know education. We went to school, we attended classes, we rule this turf—and for a long time, we've known it well enough to transfer this expertise to our children when they've needed help. For decades, our adorable offspring have sat down at the end of the school day, opened their textbooks, and tackled homework with which we could easily assist: multiplication tables, spelling words, map coloring.

But now, the educational landscape has changed. Kids don't stuff books into their backpacks, they access PDFs via their iPads and laptops. They don't call a friend to discuss an assignment, they ooVoo chums to figure it out (and socialize a bit, too). They don't type and hand in a paper, they word process it, clear it for originality through Turnitin, and then submit it online to their teacher. Multiplication and spelling quizzes? There are apps for those. And maps? Google affords learners the most up-to-date, real satellite and street maps of the entire planet—no more paper copies of mystery squiggle countries in outline. No matter what subject matter your kids are learning, there's probably a playlist of YouTube videos providing instructional help on that topic. With new technology topics you never studied in school—like coding—it's a relief to know that all those resources are available.

So where does that leave you—what is your role as an interested and engaged parent? How are you supposed to stay "in the loop" and offer support to your children when they need actual human help? It may be of worth to first acknowledge how you may be feeling about the monumental shift between how you were taught and what you know—and how your kids are being taught and what they are expected to know. If you're feeling that the change is a little scary, don't worry, you're not alone. But as Sheryl Sandberg, COO of Facebook, famously asks, "What would you do if you weren't afraid?" You would find the resources and guidance that you need in order to provide your children the help that they need. And that's where **Coding for Parents** comes in handy!

Recognizing that you are playing two roles—a learner who may be new to coding, and a guide who is seeking to assist your children—this book presents you with clear examples, easy-to-understand images, and just the right quantity of text to clarify each concept. You'll find helpful guidance that introduces you to coding in the same manner your children are being introduced to it: building gently and progressively, from simple tile languages like Scratch to web basics (including HTML and CSS), and finally to web interactivity (JavaScript).

As with many activities in which we coach our children, we learn and improve as we go. You are not expected to be an instant expert in coding, and **Coding for Parents** understands and values your concerns. There will be occasions when you'll need to work through a section, put the book down and reflect on the ideas, then return to the material later. That's OK! It won't happen too often, but know that this is normal when working to develop a completely new skill set. I encounter this situation often, and when I do, I share my concerns with my own children. The soft skills of remaining optimistic, pushing through challenges, and consulting resources (people, books, and other tools) are equally important messages to your kids as elevating coding skills. Ultimately, you and your kids will benefit from **Coding for Parents**, setting the stage for success in future technological forays we have yet to dream up!

Camille McCue, PhD

Author • Educator • Innovator

camillemccue.com

CONTENTS

INTRODUCTION // 8

The introductory section explains what coding is, as well as common uses, common misconceptions, what you will need to get started, and a simple guide to this book.

CHAPTER 1: CODING CONCEPTS // 18

Key concepts of coding are based on logic and common sense. This chapter will teach you how to think in a new way—and you won't even need a computer!

CHAPTER 2: WHAT IS SCRATCH? // 56

Scratch is a great program for beginner coders. Learn to use it to write simple code blocks in a visual format and create dynamic animations. Includes several sample projects.

CHAPTER 3: WHAT ARE HTML AND CSS? // 86

Here's where the serious coding begins! HTML code creates the structure of websites, and CSS adds decorative elements to make them look amazing. Learn to build a basic website over the course of this chapter, one element at a time.

CHAPTER 4: WHAT IS JAVASCRIPT? // 136

JavaScript is a programming language used to make web pages interactive. Learn the key elements of JavaScript, and work on sample projects for coding interactive web pages.

FURTHER LEARNING // 188

A closing section discusses areas of further study, from programming languages not covered in this book to advanced coding skills. Resources for online learning are explained, and finally some tips to encourage your coding practice—a great note to end on!

GLOSSARY // 196

INDEX // 206

ACKNOWLEDGMENTS // 208

INTRODUCTION

Learning the fundamentals of coding will allow you to help kids with their homework, while teaching you a new way to think.

This guide to coding has been written especially for parents, just like you, whose children are learning computer programming in school. Curriculum can vary, but coding is becoming increasingly important in classrooms and at home in the form of homework. If you are used to helping your children, but have no background in writing software this can seem very daunting. There is a world of terminology to grasp, and if you are out of the habit of learning, this can prove a challenge.

Rest assured, understanding the concepts behind coding—and its importance in today's world—is within your reach. This guide introduces exactly what coding is and what you need to get started. You will learn how to use **Scratch** (a great program for beginners) as well as more in-depth **HTML** and **CSS**, the building blocks for websites. Also included is an explanation of **JavaScript**, the programming language that allows interactive elements to be added, which will take your website knowledge even further.

SYMBOL KEY

Tips and inspiration

Activities and mini-tasks

Key points

Concepts and tricks to remember

One of the best ways to learn is by doing, so this guide encourages practical application of the topics covered. Throughout the book, notes, tips, and activities are included to help you add another level to your learning. Enjoy the process of developing a new skill and keep on track by referring to the glossary (terms are bolded throughout). Once you have mastered the basics, there is advice for further learning in the last chapter of the book. Children learn incredibly quickly and are used to the fast-paced nature of technology, but there is no need to be left behind—work together with your kids to develop a skill that is certain to be of use to you both in the future!

In this book, we will introduce some examples of key coding concepts to highlight the way in which a machine organizes and processes information. We will look at how mistakes can occur, how to create organized, beautiful code examples, and even build some cool animations, games, and applications using a range of coding programs. This book will provide you with a helpful introduction to coding, setting you up with a solid understanding of its key concepts and a clear starting point for further learning. In an increasingly digitized world, a grasp of coding can offer many exciting opportunities.

Children are being taught the basics of programming in schools to prepare them for today's digital culture, and it's important for the rest of us to do our best to keep up! As well as being especially helpful for imparting a base level of knowledge to inspire continued study, this book will prepare you to help young beginner coders with their homework!

Notes on an ongoing project

Parent notes

References

Diagrams and analysis

WHAT IS CODING?

Coding is a language, and also a logic-based way of thinking.

At its simplest, learning to code is simply learning to tell machines what to do. Code is the language used to give instructions to a computer for every task it performs from displaying words on a screen, to running elaborate animations. Send a text, take money from an ATM, play a video game, and you are relying on people having written the code that makes it possible.

Unlike the languages used by people to communicate with each other, which can be vague, emotional, or even irrational, coding languages are fixed, logical, and precise. They have to be, because computers take everything literally!

Imagine this scenario: you're about to ask a friend to buy you some snacks. You need to provide money, directions to the store, and a list of your favorite foods. It sounds simple, but your friend would still need to make decisions in order to succeed, considering the information you have provided. They would need to follow directions, (deciding what to do if they got lost on the way); at the store, they would have to consider each item to see if it met your criteria. They would also have to check each snack's cost against the current total of the purchase and the total amount of money they have; then they would have to complete the purchase, collect any change, and return to you.

The process would be simple enough for your friend, as these decisions can be made intuitively, but a machine has no intuition to fall back on. A coder would need to find a specific way to instruct a machine. There are values to remember (directions, money total), repeatable actions (considering snack options), and comparisons (checking price against total), making this a very tricky task indeed for a machine.

This book will introduce you to **computational thinking**, and give you the tools to program code for just this sort of task.

HOW DID WE GET HERE?

Here are some of the key milestones in the creation and development of modern coded machines.

First "thinking" machine: Calculating devices have been around since the abacus, but the first mechanical computer to complete complex sums was the difference engine completed by Charles Babbage in the early nineteenth century. Together with Ada Lovelace, he devised plans for a more advanced analytical engine, but it was never completed. Their work was the beginning of multipurpose thinking machines.

First computers: In the age of electricity, faster and more advanced machines could now be built. Some early examples are the Atanasoff–Berry computer (ABC) and ENIAC (Electronic Numerical Integrator And Computer) in the mid-twentieth century. Early computers were used to predict missile trajectory and crack coded messages during WWII.

Personal computers: Personal computers (or PCs) became available in the 1960s, but had to be programmed by hand. Later innovations from companies like Microsoft and Apple built in operating systems so it became simpler for users to complete tasks without needing to program each command manually.

The Internet: Eventually machines were able to connect and share information in networks, which led to the Internet emerging in the early 1990s.

Modern innovations: Computers began as large and inefficient machines, but can now load music, videos, and games remotely on small portable phones. The future could see intelligent machines integrated into everyday items—or even human beings—to make our lives easier.

USES OF CODING

Computer code is an integral part of the modern world, and learning to understand it will give you many advantages.

Computer code underlies the function of so many of the machines we take for granted. It takes many forms and performs many functions from running **hardware** like computers, ATMs, and airplanes to **software** like apps and operating systems. People who work with code are usually called coders, programmers, or developers, but as the technology of the world evolves, so do the uses of coding skills. People in all industries can benefit from learning these skills, and so can schoolchildren.

KIDS WHO CODE

Like everything, coding is actually easier to learn for children than for adults—the key is to understand computational thinking, and to grasp what is possible within its frameworks. It really is like learning a new language!

All that's required to learn coding is a grasp of logic. The program Scratch, covered in Chapter 2, was originally designed for kids eight and up, but can be used by younger children (basic reading is required, and adult supervision or parental controls are recommended for young children using the Internet). The later chapters of this book focus on HTML, CSS, and JavaScript, which are very detail-oriented and can be frustrating for younger children (and adult beginners!), but certainly not impossible.

Coding is a fantastic skill, well worth learning at any age!

GET KIDS EXCITED ABOUT CAREER OPTIONS

Skills in coding are increasingly valuable as advances in technology and computing produce greater demand. If kids find coding an exciting and challenging hobby then it could be worth encouraging them to think about careers that involve coding tasks—and there are all kinds!

Web development

There are many creative careers relating to building and maintaining websites and applications, from designing the interface and user experience to implementing web pages using logic and testing.

Gaming

The gaming industry is huge and varied with many careers for people to write, build, and test new projects. Modern games are usually complex with detailed graphics, but just like the simple projects we will learn to build in this book, they need to follow logical steps and avoid errors.

Software

Browsers are used to run our web code, but the browsers themselves are built with code! Beyond the web, computer software and operating systems are always in need of coders to keep them updated.

AI

AI (artificial intelligence) is the programming of machines to absorb, process, and make decisions based on **input**. This can take many forms, like autonomous, driverless cars and voice-automated assistant programs.

Data science

Using large amounts of input data, statistical analysis can provide insight into trends and behaviors. Using supercomputers, which are large-capacity and fast processing machines, many records can be processed so that data scientists can predict otherwise unpredictable outcomes, for example the financial market.

MISCONCEPTIONS ABOUT CODING

Here are some common myths that might put you off encouraging your kids to code—let's dispel them!

 Myth: You need to be really good at math

Truth: A page of complicated code might look similar to a page of sums and equations, leading many to think the two are similar. Coding can require you to think in a logical, structured way and can involve numbers, but you don't necessarily need to be good at math to learn to code. There are crossovers with math such as the focus on problem-solving and the use of representative numbers, but there are no mathematical prerequisites to learning code.

 Myth: Coding is boring and not creative

Truth: Compared to arts subjects, it is easy to see why coding can seem dull and uninspiring. An initial glance at a page of code seems dry compared to photos, paintings, or sculpture, but coding can be incredibly imaginative. Not only can coding be used to create beautiful games and applications, but functional, interactive content completely hand-tailored by their creator. The process of coding can be an addictively entertaining hobby that involves solving problems with a creative mindset. It just takes a little understanding.

Myth: You need expensive computers and software

Truth: Nope. Fast, modern computers are necessary for some art and video software and that need high processing power and memory, but code itself is just text. A PC or laptop with a text editor program and a browser is sufficient to get started—you don't even need an Internet connection!

 Myth: It's really complicated

Truth: Like most subjects, coding does become more complicated as you progress and learn more, but this shouldn't be a block to getting started. A glance at a page of complex code may appear daunting to a beginner, but don't worry, we will start small. This book begins at the ground level to introduce concepts, then gradually builds toward simple code blocks and eventually some more involved code, giving every new addition a context and explanation. By the time you get to the end, that page of code might not seem so complicated after all!

 Myth: It's a very lonely activity

Truth: Often when people think of a computer programmer, they imagine a geeky person coding alone in their room—but this just isn't true! A great deal of learning involves seeking help, either by searching online or testing your projects with friends and family. Coding with friends is an effective strategy and joining (or setting up) study groups is common practice to keep you motivated and improving. Coding is about building things to be used by others, so it is important to introduce a social element to your work, even if it's just sharing to get feedback.

GETTING STARTED

As with any new skill, it's important to start at the beginning and build your knowledge.

There are many ways that you could approach learning to code. A large percentage of professional developers are entirely or partly self-taught, as the field is so new and these skills have only recently been deemed teachable. Learning through necessity is effective, but it will give you the skills to perform only specific tasks and could leave gaps in your understanding, so we will begin with the basics.

By beginning with the concepts that coding is built upon, you can focus on what the code does, rather than worrying about the format. Once we have covered the logic, we will look at Scratch software, which is designed to easily introduce computational thinking. From there we will begin to look at hand-typed code with HTML and CSS web pages, then finally, we will explore the use of JavaScript to alter the inputs and behavior of web pages. With this progression from thought to tools and software, you will hopefully appreciate the fundamentals and gain a solid understanding of coding, which will help you take on new tools—and confidently build your own projects.

SETTING UP

Our opening chapter does not require any software, though you may want to take notes or draw out your own **algorithms** on paper. For the later chapters you will need a computer to complete the exercises. You will need an Internet connection to access Scratch for Chapter 2, as well as an email address to sign up, but the software is free. You will also need a simple HTML **text editor** program to complete Chapters 3 and 4. These are also free to download, and we have suggested several options.

TABLET OR COMPUTER?

You could use a tablet to follow along with this book, but you may find it more difficult in the later coding chapters, which require heavy amounts of typing and symbols (such as </"|>) that could be difficult on a tablet. The process of saving and refreshing web pages requires frequent jumping between applications, which can also be harder on a tablet. A laptop or PC will be the best tool for coding.

GOOD CODING BEHAVIORS

As we will discover in this book, there are some behaviors, general policies, and attributes of writing effective code. Some of these will involve the formatting and simplification of the code itself, but also attention to detail and commitment to making things work correctly. Try to avoid directly copying examples from the book without first examining what is happening and why. This will keep you thinking creatively and actively learning, which are both key to becoming a great coder!

CODING CONCEPTS

Get to grips with coding—without the code!

In this chapter we are not going to use any specific code—we don't even need a computer, only basic logic. To begin with, we will look at some of the ideas and concepts commonly used in coding and explain why a computer "thinks" or functions in a certain way. These key concepts will explain the necessity and the primary function of code—understanding the why of code makes it a lot easier to learn the how!

IN THIS CHAPTER WE WILL COVER:

- **Algorithms**
- **Conditional flow**
- **Variables** and their four main types
- Ways to be effective and efficient
- Testing and solving problems

COMPUTER-FREE CODING

You will not need a computer or any software for this chapter, as we are looking at ideas rather than direct code. You may need a pencil and paper to follow mini-challenges and try drawing your own **functions**.

PROGRAMMING LANGUAGES

There are many different programming languages (such as **HTML, JavaScript**, etc.). Once you've learned one, it will be easier to pick up a second programming language, as they are based on similar concepts. Learning the core basics independently of a particular language or software should make it easier to take on any programming language you choose. It may also be helpful to refer back to this chapter when we begin coding in later chapters.

 Building blocks

The core concepts, or building blocks of coding (such as **loops, functions, conditions**, and **variables**) are used similarly by different programming languages and software.

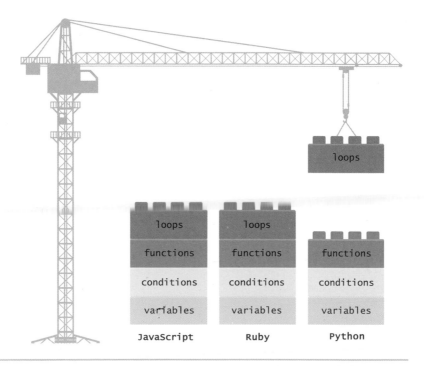

UNDERSTANDING ALGORITHMS

The algorithm is essentially a set of directions for completing a task. It is the necessary foundation of all code functions.

Algorithm is a term often used with regards to computers, but it's really just a list of ordered instructions. You could create an algorithm to explain how to complete any task—making a cup of coffee, finding a location, or even a dance routine. An algorithm is useful when the order that tasks are completed in is important and a description might be too confusing. As computers are logical and need strict instructions, code is generally written in algorithms so that the computer can understand what it is supposed to do and work as expected.

 Algorithm: Getting Ready in the Morning

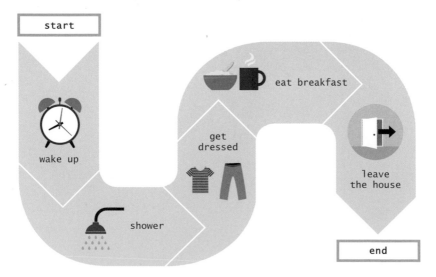

RULES OF THE ALGORITHM

Define start and end points

Make sure there is a clearly defined start and end point, so the program cannot start from anywhere but the first step, and it's clear when the instructions have been completed.

One at a time

Each step must be completed before you can start the next. Algorithms don't allow for multitasking, although you can write a single step that includes multiple actions.

Values needed

Most instructions are either done or not done, but some might require additional inputs. For example, a functional algorithm would have to define "eating breakfast" for a computer.

Conditional flow

Steps must proceed in order as conditions are met—you must get dressed before you can leave the house, for example!

 WHO IS IT FOR?

In coding, algorithms are written for computers, but in this chapter you are following the algorithm, so the text may refer to "you," rather than "the program."

 MINI TASK

Parents, try to write your own algorithm for a daily routine. Use the main diagram as a guide and make sure everything works in the correct order (it should probably start with "wake up" and end with "go to sleep.")

MORE ALGORITHMS

To create more complex algorithms capable of performing complicated tasks, we will need to add options for customization.

Another reason the algorithm is ideal for telling computers what to do, is that it can offer options, allowing the computer to make decisions and calculate information. This means that the same algorithm can work in lots of situations with different **inputs** (information provided by **users**) and solve different problems. Clever algorithms that can do repeatable tasks, but not always the exact same way, are a vital reason why computers are so efficient and powerful.

⚙ **Algorithm: Making Coffee**

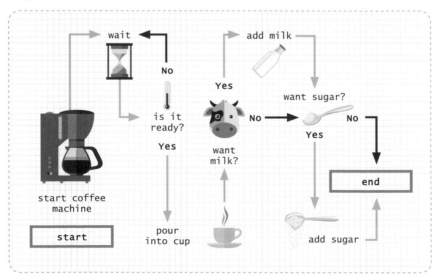

MORE RULES OF ALGORITHMS

The "Making Coffee" algorithm uses some additional rules to vary the final **output**.

Loops

A waiting step is called a **loop** and in this example, ensures the coffee is not poured until it's ready.

Flow

In this diagram, arrows, representing **flow**, take the program to the next step. There is always a next step so the algorithm continues to flow until it gets to the end.

Keep the order

The sequence of events is important. Just look at the getting-ready algorithm—you wouldn't put your clothes on before getting in the shower, would you?

Conditionals

Some steps are called **conditionals.** They are points of diversion, where the user must make a choice that affects the eventual outcome.

End

As before, it is important that despite the options chosen, the algorithm always reaches completion at the end step.

CONDITIONS

Conditions are the tools necessary for a computer to make decisions and run algorithms and programs.

In the last section, our coffee-making algorithm posed a choice with optional steps for adding milk and sugar, and instructions for proceeding based on "yes" or "no" answers. This is called **conditional flow** (where flow refers to the steps of the algorithm being completed in their designated order). Sometimes in coding, the program may need to make decisions, and if that's the case, it needs to know clearly how to do this. Conditions will tell your program how to make a decision, and how to proceed in every possible eventuality.

IF/ELSE

An **if/else statement** is a type of **conditional** that instructs a program what to do if it passes a requirement, or alternatively what to do if it fails. In the diagram on the opposite page, we use a series of questions and if/else branching to guess what type of pet you might have. At every decision-making point, there is an option given if the statement is accepted, and another option in case it is not.

AND/OR

If you are checking for multiple things, you may check a combination using **and/or values**. Using "and" will do something if both conditions are met. Using "or" will do something if one of the conditions is met. Using these together will allow for a more powerful ability to query information.

What pet do you have?

Follow the questions and the flow diagram will guess your answer!

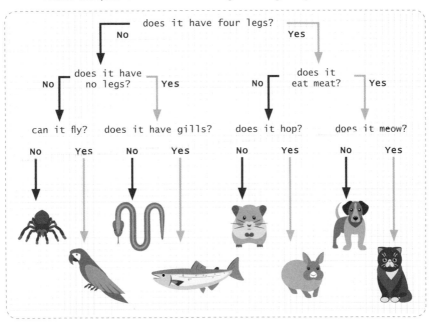

 ## GO WITH THE FLOW

Remember: there should always be a plan for what to do in every scenario. If the algorithm doesn't know what to do (for example, if the person guessing doesn't actually have a pet) there is no route to proceed, it cannot finish and the flow will be broken.

MINI TASK

Using the flow chart, work out which animals will be found for the following queries:

- Has 2 legs, can fly OR cannot fly
- Has 4 legs AND eats meat
- Does not have 4 legs AND can fly OR has gills

LOOPS

Looping is an essential tool for repeating tasks and finding information by repeating the same code a set number of times.

One of the benefits of algorithms is that they can be repeated over and over automatically as part of the flow, rather than having to stop and repeat the same instructions manually each time. Sometimes, we may want to set a task to repeat a certain number of times, and for this we use **loops**. Loops involve specifying a task that can then be repeated. Once we have defined the task, we can refer back to it quickly, making our algorithms even more efficient.

 Looped algorithm: Mail Delivery

An algorithm for a mailman gives a task list (called a **function**) for delivering mail, then uses loops, so the delivery task list is repeated at each house. This saves us from having to give the same set of instructions for each house along the route. See the task list on the left, and the outcome on the right.

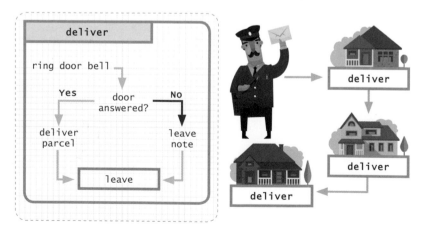

USING LOOPS FOR OUTPUT

Using **dynamic values** (which can be edited) we can write an algorithm to reduce a list of instructions to one instruction that contains loops. For example, to instruct a program to complete a repetitive numerical task, you could create an algorithm that loops for every number in a set range.

⚙ **Looped algorithm: Writing Your Times Tables**

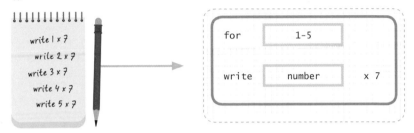

USING LOOPS TO SEARCH

To search for information, we can write an algorithm to check through items in a list until it finds the value it is looking for. For efficiency, we would set a loop to check every item on the list, but to stop once the correct answer is found, even if there are still items which have not been checked.

⚙ **Looped algorithm: Find Cleo**

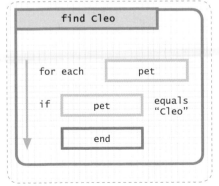

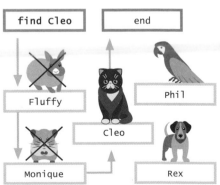

FUNCTIONS

It's time to upgrade our algorithms into functions by adding some code-specific elements.

A **function** is a coding term meaning a repeatable task, which can calculate information and output results based on different inputs. This may sound very similar to an algorithm, and that's because a function is a type of algorithm, but while algorithms aren't specifically related to computing, functions are. They use specific tools such as **variables** that we will use in our coding, so we will be working with functions from now on.

Functions are essentially saved blocks of information that can be called upon when needed. They also take in specific values called **parameters** (usually given as a choice between options), which can be used in the function's calculations and decision-making. On the opposite page, our coffee-making algorithm (see page 22) has been adapted into a programming function. We have added more options, so users can now specify a type of drink, what, if anything, to add to it, and whether they take sugar. See the function diagram opposite, and annotations below.

⚙ **"Make a Drink" function elements**

① By giving the function an identifiable name "Make a Drink," we will recognize it easily and can reuse it as needed.

② Our check "is it ready" will now loop until the water is ready. If the check comes back negative (i.e., the water is not hot enough) the function will wait one minute, then start over. The second "make drink" line shows the function being called again within the function, starting itself over.

③ The green boxes represent parameters, which are set by the user. So in this function you could specify a different type of drink: tea, or cocoa, for example. Here you specify what the variable "drink" means in the function.

⚙ Function: Make a Drink

KEY

| functions | variables | parameters | end |

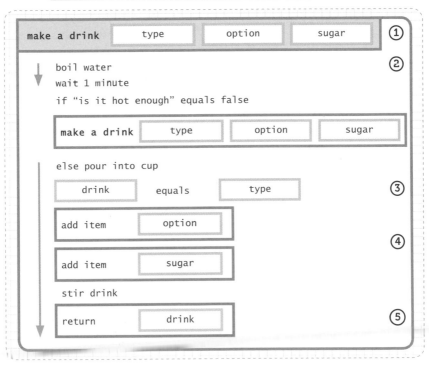

make a drink | type | option | sugar | ①

② boil water
wait 1 minute
if "is it hot enough" equals false

make a drink | type | option | sugar |

else pour into cup

drink | equals | type | ③

add item | option |

④

add item | sugar |

stir drink

return | drink | ⑤

④ We can also make functions to run inside of functions (**nested functions**), so any similar code can be **minified** for simplicity. Here we have separated the adding of items like milk and sugar into separate functions, which can be called as needed to give us more control.

⑤ We end the function with a **return**, which is the end result of our function—our answer. In this case the return is our completed drink.

VARIABLES

Variables are stored values that can be inserted into functions. You can think of a variable as a container for information.

So far we have made our functions work by analyzing the information directly entered into them as **parameters** (such as milk and sugars), but sometimes we may need to make our own values to analyze. Using **variables** we can create values that a function remembers and can change based on what happens. A variable could be used in a game, for example to check the user's score or keep track of levels. A variable can also be a useful way to create a setting, meaning you would only need to change one value rather than many.

 Value variables

The variable "dogs" is a saved list of dogs that is updated when we apply functions to it, as below. The function "add dog (name)" will add another dog to the information stored in the original variable "dogs."

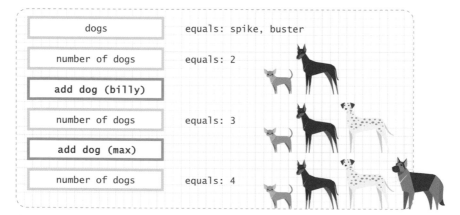

dogs	equals: spike, buster
number of dogs	equals: 2
add dog (billy)	
number of dogs	equals: 3
add dog (max)	
number of dogs	equals: 4

VARIABLE TYPES

Variables can be **inputs** (values added by users) or even combinations of other variables. Many types of function can be carried out on variables based on their type. The next pages will look at four types of variable.

⚙ **Input variables**

"First" and "second" are input variables, and "full name" is a combination of two variables. Editing either of the input variables will update "full name."

⚙ **Reusing a variable**

Another benefit of variables is the fact that they can be reused. By making a variable for a character's name in a story, for example, we can edit the variable to change the name throughout the story, rather than manually changing each instance. This is an example of a **config value**.

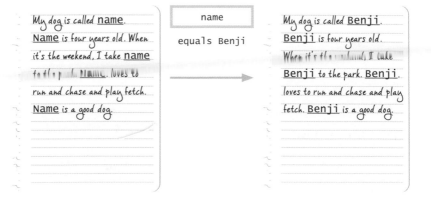

INTEGERS AND BOOLEANS

Two common variable types are integers (numbers) and Booleans (true/false values).

In the last section we introduced the concept of variables and what they can be used for. Different variable types can provide functions with different capabilities, so it's worth discussing them in more depth. **Integers** and **Booleans** are two key types of variables used in coding.

INTEGERS

Simply put, integers are variables for whole numbers. Setting a variable integer is obviously helpful for tracking a number in your code (such as the quantity of something or how many times an action should be performed) and integers allow you to make mathematical changes through functions (such as addition/subtraction).

Numbers can also be used for checking if something has reached a maximum or minimum value, or if it is equal to a certain numerical requirement. Setting integer variables is also a key component of algebra, where the character x is most commonly used to represent the variable.

⚙ **Variables in algebra**

The equations below show how variables are used in simple algebra, but they can be used for much more complex math, and more.

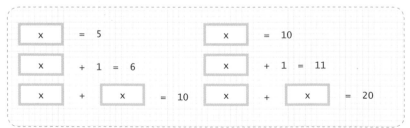

BOOLEANS

Booleans are the simplest variable type as there are only two possible values: true or false. A Boolean value will always be either true or false, making it ideal for something you need to set as on or off, done or not done. While this may seem limiting compared to numbers or text, it's sometimes very helpful to make a simple switch variable with a clear status (such as adding milk or not in our coffee-making algorithm on page 22).

Functions can use Boolean variables to identify all the true statements from a list, or to return a list of tasks that still need to be done. They are a useful tool for sorting data. In the diagram on page 32, you could use a function to query whether "x" is greater than 4, or divisible by 5, and the return would be either true or false; a Boolean value.

⚙ Using Boolean values to sort data

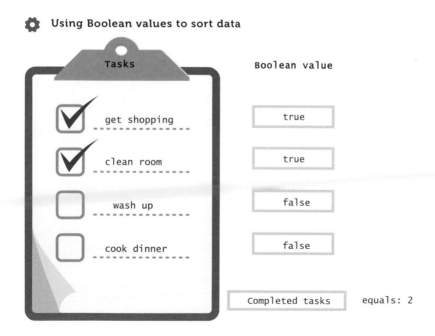

Tasks	Boolean value
✓ get shopping	true
✓ clean room	true
☐ wash up	false
☐ cook dinner	false

Completed tasks   equals: 2

STRINGS AND LISTS

Variables can be text, or even combinations of other variables, allowing you to set up even more complex types of function.

STRINGS

Strings are variables made up of text values. You may use a text variable for a name or label, and you could perform functions on a string to check its length (how many text characters it has), change the text (such as convert to all capitals), or combine with other strings. If you refer back to our "Make a Drink" function (page 29), the variable "drink" has to be set to a parameter, "type," which could be a value like coffee, tea, cocoa, etc. These are all examples of string variables.

LISTS

The final variable type we will look at is **lists** (sometimes called **arrays**). Lists can be combinations of string, integer, and Boolean values, and are helpful for storing a sequence of information. Functions can use list variables to check their length and add and remove things from them, as well as checking for specific items using a loop, or requesting an **index** from the list. This is all very helpful for organizing and presenting data.

▱▸ **PRACTICE MAKES PERFECT**

Parents, this is a good topic to practice until kids can identify variable types automatically. Try identifying examples of each type in a newspaper page, highlighting each in a different color. Once you start noticing them, you'll see variable types everywhere!

⚙ **Identifying variable types**

Different variable types allow functions to use their information to check different things. Take a look at the variables below, which include all the types we have discussed. With all these variables, you could build a detailed function. You can check if the name is too long because it is a string, you can check the age is not too old as it is an integer. You can check if the person owns a pet because it is a Boolean, and you can check how many pets because the value is a list. You could also query the list variable to find out how many pets there are, and check there aren't too many, or find a specific entry (for example, the third pet is "Spots").

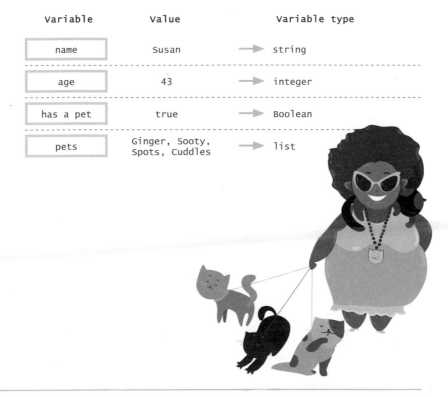

variable	Value	Variable type
name	Susan	→ string
age	43	→ integer
has a pet	true	→ Boolean
pets	Ginger, Sooty, Spots, Cuddles	→ list

USER INPUTS

Input values are provided by the user, which present their own unique challenges.

The **user** is whoever your code is built for, and **user input** means any information or interaction that the user provides. For example, in a game the user might press a button or select an option, or on a website the user might fill in a form—these are all types of user input. Earlier we looked at parameters, such as how a user can specify options when calling a function (i.e. coffee with milk and two sugars). This is an example of user input as the user is specifying inputs to determine how the function will work.

One of the challenges of user inputs is that you cannot predict what a user might do or what inputs a user might provide, and will need to prepare responses for all possible outcomes.

Even a question that's simple to ask aloud becomes much more complicated when you realize that you have to write a function that can process all kinds of possible answers!

 Accounting for user input

The "How Many Pets" function on the opposite page processes user input to try to create the variable "answer" as an integer variable—meaning it should answer the question "how many pets?" with a number. But it must account for a wide variety of answer types in order to be effective. Imagine all the things people could come up with:

⚙ Function: How Many Pets?

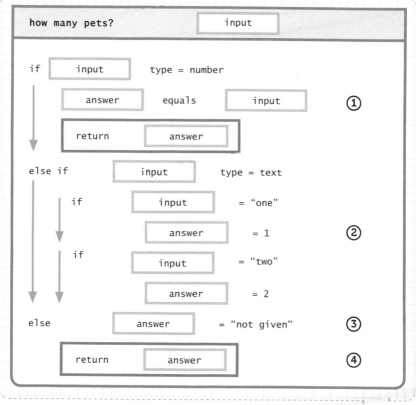

how many pets? | input

if | input | type = number
     answer equals input ①
     return answer

else if | input | type = text
     if | input | = "one"
       answer = 1 ②
     if | input | = "two"
       answer = 2

else | answer | = "not given" ③

return answer ④

① First we check if the input is a number, and if so We return that value as the answer.

② If not we check if it is text, then try to convert that text to a number. The function should be prepared for likely text answers.

③ If the variable cannot be identified as either number or text, then the function will return with the answer "not given."

④ Note the paths always lead to the end, this way the function never gets stuck and always completes.

DON'T REPEAT YOURSELF (DRY)

The phrase "don't repeat yourself," or DRY, is a key philosophy for successful coding, meant to remind you to always reduce your code to the simplest possible form.

One of the benefits of coding functions is their ability to repeat tasks, meaning you don't have to manually repeat the same request each time. Making a smaller, repeatable code has a number of benefits that make it easier for both you and the computer. First, the computer has less to remember and will always reliably do the same thing. Also, because you are writing less code, there is less risk of you making mistakes. Finally, it is easier to make alterations to your code.

This also helps you build new things faster because you can include functions you have already written rather than having to write everything from scratch. The **DRY** philosophy is an important concept in coding and we should always try to stick to it where possible. If you feel a task is repeating the same steps frequently, that might be an indication that a repeatable function could make your code more efficient.

Say you want to write out a function to buy snacks. If you are a snacker, this could quite quickly get out of hand. For every snack item, you have to go to the store, pick your snack, buy your snack, then come home—that's four steps per snack!

NOW LET'S SIMPLIFY!

To simplify a repetitive function, ask yourself what its key components are—what is accomplished? Then identify the pattern and which steps are consistently being repeated.

In the example of a snack function, we are clearly looking to create a function for buying food, and the steps in the process—such as going to the store and looking for each item—apply equally to each separate food item. Therefore the unique steps in the list can be reduced to the actual snack items you want, for example:

1. Get a drink
2. Get a pizza
3. Get an ice cream

The ideal solution is a dynamic function, with the snack as a parameter.

 "Buy a" function

Now, we can just call this function and it will repeat the tasks for the specified product. If you were writing a function for your whole day, you could incorporate this function as needed with minimal effort.

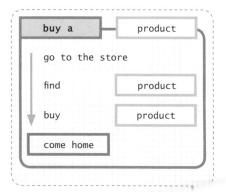

```
buy a          product

go to the store

find           product

buy            product

come home
```

 REDUCE, REUSE, REFACTOR

The process of refining code by breaking it into smaller functions like this is called code **refactoring.** Parents, it's a great idea to keep track of the new vocabulary terms we're learning and make a set of flashcards.

KEEP IT SIMPLE, STUPID (KISS)

The phrase "keep it simple, stupid," or KISS, is similar to DRY, but is more focused on planning and problem solving.

Coding is a process of telling a computer to complete a task, and we should always aim to do this in the shortest and simplest way. In the last section, we saw how using a DRY philosophy can simplify our code, but if we plan correctly from the start and use **computational thinking**, we can write clean and simple code. Bear **KISS** in mind as you progress, to ensure that your code is as straightforward and functional as possible.

⚙ **The simplest "Set Age" function**

Here we cut out the middle step of specifying possible answers, and directly return the input as the age, meaning less chance of errors.

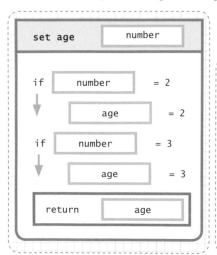

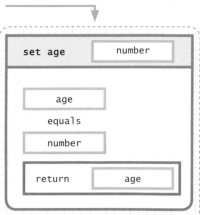

⚙ The simplest "Find My Pet" function

We want to create a function to find my dog, "Spike." The first attempt
focuses on various details, and requires three parameters to be confirmed
to come to a conclusion. The reduced option uses the quickest and easiest
function to solve the problem, based on the information we have available.
Since we know his name, let's just search for that. This function has been
simplified based on logic rather than tidying code.

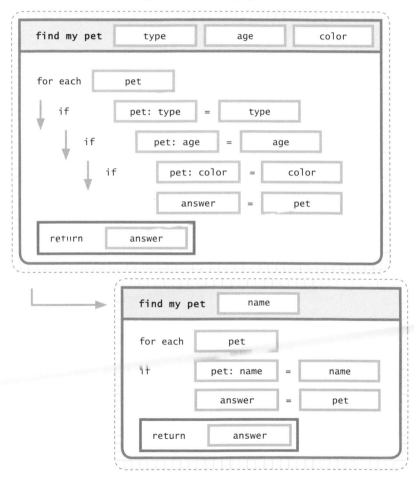

DEBUGGING

Debugging means investigating problems and trying to resolve them, a sometimes frustrating—but essential—skill in coding.

The term **debugging** comes from the early days of computing when machines were as big as entire rooms. Bugs would fly into the electronics and break the machines, meaning people would need to remove the bugs to fix it. Nowadays a **bug** means an **error** that stops your code working as expected, and debugging is the process of fixing it.

Quite often, a bug is a combination of making a mistake in the code and the computer doing the wrong thing (because it has been instructed to), but there could also be a fault with the software or **hardware** that cannot be fixed in the code. Debugging is the process of finding out where and what the problem is.

Once you have checked for basic typos and errors in structure, if the code still isn't behaving as expected, try asking yourself these questions:

1. What makes you think your code isn't working?

2. What did you expect your code to do and why?

3. What did your code do instead, and how do you know?

 LEARN AS YOU GO

Your process of debugging might change each time depending on the type of problem, but it is a valuable skill to be able to understand code and interpret where mistakes might be happening.

 KEY POINT

Every programmer, from beginner to expert level, will spend a large portion of their time debugging, so don't feel frustrated by this step.

DEBUGGING A SAMPLE FUNCTION

This function lets you input your age to see if you are old enough to watch an R-rated movie, but it has wrongly allowed someone who is too young to see the film. We need to debug the function!

⚙ **Steps for debugging**

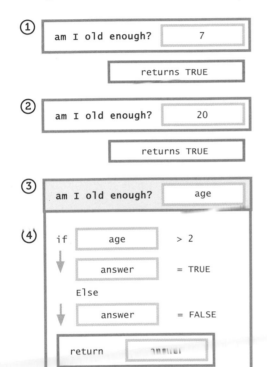

(1) am I old enough? | 7

returns TRUE

(2) am I old enough? | 20

returns TRUE

(3) am I old enough? | age

(4)
```
if    age    > 2
        answer    = TRUE
    Else
        answer    = FALSE
    return    answer
```

(1) Check the output. The fact we are receiving a response means that some part of the function is working. If no response was returned we would suspect the problem to be a broken function flow.

(2) Test a different input. By changing the input value we can see if the response changes. (If we test with an older age and receive a no, we would know the function is giving opposite answers.)

(3) Read through the function step-by-step to see what could be happening each time—you might spot what is going wrong.

(4) Aha! It seems we have entered the wrong number to check against our age input. Let's change it to 13.

(5) Test. Now lets test our function is working as expected. It is! The bug has been fixed.

am I old enough? | 7

(5) returns FALSE

CODE MANAGEMENT

We have all the tools to begin coding, but need to bear in mind how to maintain and manage this code.

When working on a project it's easy to get carried away and end up writing a large amount of code. While this is not necessarily a problem, if you don't keep it easy to read and understand, it can create problems later on, such as incorporating errors. You may find it easier to break your code into sections, making it more transparent and easier to check. You may also want to write notes for yourself to help remind you what is happening in your code.

⚙ Best practices

Take a look at the opposite page. This is our "Make a Drink" function from page 29, but reduced and organized to its simplest form.

① **Add comments:** Most software will allow you to add comments to functions so you can label different elements. This will not be read by the computer or change the code, but will help you and other readers to understand the code better.

② **Give descriptive names:** Another way to make it easy for you to remember what the code does is with clear descriptive names for your functions and variables. It is obvious the function "add milk" will probably add the milk.

③ **Clean display:** Another way to make code cleaner is with visual spacing and **indentation**. This way we can see which functions belong together. This will not make the code any better in functionality, but will make it easier for humans to use.

④ **Arrange by type:** By putting similar sections together, we can easily find the relevant part to work on. Here all the function calls are grouped together, so we don't need to find where each call is being made throughout the code.

⚙ **Well-managed code: "Make a Drink" function**

① //Function definition

② | make a drink | type | option | sugar |

> boil water
> wait 1 minute
> if "is it hot enough" equals false

| make a drink | type | option | sugar |

else pour into cup

| drink | = | type |

③

if | option |

| add | option |

if | sugar |

| add | sugar |

stir | drink |

| return | drink |

① //Sample function calls

④ | make a drink | coffee | milk | 2 |

| make a drink | tea | milk | 2 |

| make drink | tea | cream | 0 |

COMMON CODING ISSUES

Here are a few mistakes coders often make while building projects. Remember these errors to avoid potential pitfalls.

 I don't know what is causing the problem

You may find an issue with your code not working, but not know where it's happening. This might be a sign that your functions are too large and complicated, and could use some simplification and refactoring. See page 40 for tips on keeping code simple.

 My variable isn't recording the correct value

You may have used the same variable more than once. Variables need to be kept unique or your code could become confused. Keep them distinctly named and descriptive as to what information they hold. If your variable isn't showing any information at all, you may have spelled it differently or used spaces or capital letters, so your variables do not match throughout the function.

My function is not doing what I expected

You might find the outputs or results of your code are not working in the way you wanted, meaning you have a bug in your code. Not to worry, debugging is an essential skill to coding and is an opportunity to learn. Looking at the result of your code may provide a clue as to what's wrong with the code, see page 42 for more debugging advice.

 My function isn't doing anything

Perhaps your code isn't doing anything at all and there is no response when you test it. This could be a number of things, but maybe it's simply because it's coded to not do anything in some circumstances. It is important that your functions are able to handle all outcomes as otherwise it will confuse you by returning nothing. You must also be careful that your code doesn't get trapped in never-ending loops and flows.

 There is no way to do what I want my code to do

You may become frustrated that you don't know how to solve a problem or do something with code, and the problem may be you are limiting yourself by what you know. If you feel you are devising overly elaborate or complicated ways to do something, there may be a simpler way that you are not aware of. It's important to keep learning and to challenge yourself to find ways to simplify your code by researching other solutions.

PROJECT 1: FASHIONBOT

Time to test your understanding by developing a function to help you choose what to wear.

We have covered many of the important concepts and skills for coding, but now it's time to begin your own code thinking. Over the next few pages, you will find projects which need adaptations and enhancements. The best way to learn is by doing, so follow along with these challenges to design your new functions.

 FashionBot

Help find the ideal outfit with our new FashionBot function (opposite). This function allows you to enter two parameters: the weather outside and your destination, and returns the list variable "clothing," telling you what to wear today. The function works so far, but requires some adjustments:

```
FashionBot[rain, park]
    Returns "raincoat, rubber boots"
FashionBot[dry, school]
    Returns "school uniform, shoes"
```

FashionBot elements

(1) Here we name our function and two parameters.

(2) Here we use conditional flow to check for rain and set the clothes variable.

(3) In the "else" section we give alternatives, so the variable "clothes" will always be set and return something.

(4) Finally, we return whatever the "clothes" is set to and end the function.

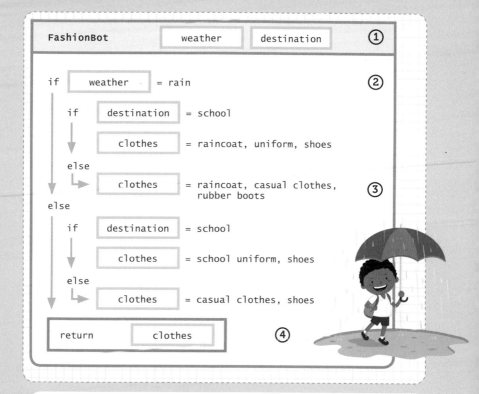

FashionBot | weather | destination | ①

```
if    weather    = rain                                    ②
    if    destination    = school
             clothes    = raincoat, uniform, shoes
    else
             clothes    = raincoat, casual clothes,         ③
                          rubber boots
else
    if    destination    = school
             clothes    = school uniform, shoes
    else
             clothes    = casual clothes, shoes

return          clothes                                     ④
```

IMPROVE OUR FUNCTION

Draw out a copy of this function, but add these changes to make it better:

Add new conditions for if weather is equal to "sunny" and add sunglasses to the "clothes" list variable.

- Add a new third parameter for hat, if hat is equal to true and destination is not equal to school then add hat to the list variable "clothes."

- Add an option that if destination is equal to "stay home" then return only "pajamas" as the variable "clothes."

PROJECT 2:
FIND THE WIZARD

Another challenge for your functional thinking, help us find the right wizard!

On the opposite page, you will find a collection of cards detailing three wizards. Each has a name, special power, and may or may not use dark magic. We built a function to retrieve the correct wizard based on their power, but some customizations would really help!

⚙ **Wizard function elements**

① Here we name our function and single parameters.

② Here we loop through the wizards to check if their power matches the one requested. If we find a match, we set the "answer" variable and return it to end the function.

③ If the power requested cannot be matched, we simply set the "answer" variable to "not found" and return that instead.

IMPROVE OUR FUNCTION

Again, draw a copy of this function with these changes to make it better:

- Create a new wizard to be included in our list. Give them a name and power and set their dark magic to true or false. What function would you need to call to retrieve your wizard?

- Imagine there were two wizards with the same power—can you find a way to search for the wizard by name instead?

- We don't want our function to allow wizards with dark magic anymore, so if the wizard found has dark magic set to true, then instead set your "answer" variable to "not allowed."

name: Alatar
power: Fire
dark magic: false

name: Glindor
power: Ice
dark magic: false

name: Noirin
power: Earth
dark magic: true

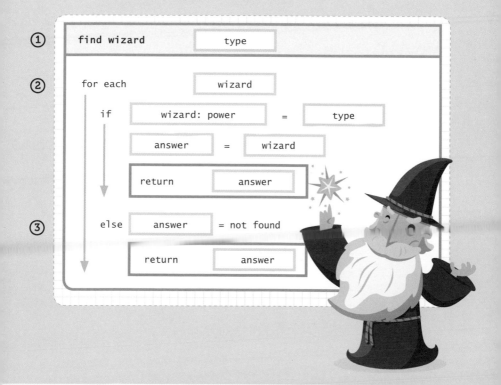

① find wizard | type

② for each | wizard

    if | wizard: power | = | type

    answer | = | wizard

    return | answer

③ else | answer | = not found

    return | answer

PROJECT 3: CAN I BUY?

In our final challenge for this chapter, use our new function to see if you can afford items in the store.

In this function (see opposite page), we simply want a yes or no answer to check if we can afford to purchase an item from the store. We supply two parameters; the item we want to buy and how much money we have. There are some challenges to improve the function, but first we must fix the error to make it work properly.

 "Can I Buy" function elements

① Here we name our function and two parameters.

② Next, we loop through the products to find the one requested.

③ Here we check the product price is less than our money, and if so we return true.

IMPROVE OUR FUNCTION

Once more, draw out the function with these improvements:

- First, we need to fix the error. It seems we return true if the user can afford the product, but do nothing if they cannot. Set an "else" to return false if the user cannot afford the product.

- Users cannot buy items when they are sold out. Check if the item is sold out and if so return false for user.

- Add the option for users to check if they can buy a quantity of product. This would involve adding a "quantity" parameter and creating a new variable that is equal to the product price multiplied by the quantity.

name: cola
price: $1
sold out: false

name: pen
price: $2
sold out: true

name: sneakers
price: $20
sold out: false

name: ice cream
price: $3
sold out: false

name: goldfish
price: $2.50
sold out: false

name: cereal
price:$2
sold out: false

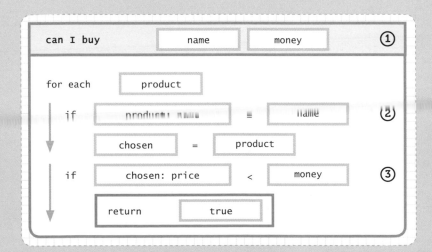

can I buy   [name]   [money]   ①

for each   [product]

  if   [product: name]   =   [name]   ②

    [chosen]   =   [product]

  if   [chosen: price]   <   [money]   ③

    [return   [true]]

SUMMARY OF CODING CONCEPTS

What have we learned in this chapter?

Congratulations on reaching the end of our coding concepts chapter. It may not seem like you have been learning code, as we have not been working on computers, but we have discussed some important rules and structures that will be valuable tools for good coding practice. The terminology and structure of these concepts, such as **functions**, **variables**, **loops**, **parameters**, and **conditions** may vary between languages and appear differently to how they are described in this chapter, but they are essentially the same in what they do and how they work. You may want to refer to the topics in this chapter later on when you begin learning to code in any language, as the principles and tips will still apply.

 REMEMBER

- Algorithms are ordered lists of instructions ideal for communicating with computers.
- A function is an algorithm with inputs and a final output based on decisions in the flow.
- Variables are temporary values set in your code to analyze and calculate outputs from.
- Debugging is a process of determining and fixing issues in your code.
- Remember to reuse code where possible and keep your code clean and easy to maintain.

5 TIPS FOR YOUR CODING PROJECTS

(1) **Plan your flow:** As we have seen throughout this
chapter, always plan out your functions' flow and ensure
there is a plan for every instance and possible outcome.
Not preparing for each input can create errors or leave users
confused by not seeing any response.

(2) **Watch out for endless loops:** Avoid an instance where a
function could endlessly loop on itself, such as constantly
searching for a non-existing item or constantly resetting to
check the same conditions. Be careful to make sure that any
loop will always result in an outcome.

(3) **Use variables:** Use variables where useful, but not as a
rule. Consider whether the variable needs to be referred to
elsewhere, or if it will need to be checked by another part of
the function. If not, you may not need to create a variable and
perhaps it would be simpler to return a simple value (like true
or false). Always use logic to decide.

(4) **Test and debug:** Remember to test your code often. It will
mean you can spot errors quicker and remain efficient while
you build your projects.

(5) **Have fun:** Remember to have fun—this means focusing on
projects that interest you and not getting too bogged down in
boring details. When you are enjoying coding, you will be much
more motivated to learn and progress.

WHAT IS SCRATCH?

Scratch is a free programming software, available online, and a fantastic tool for getting started with coding.

In the last chapter we reviewed some important coding ideas and were able to build some **functions** using them, but now it's time to put those ideas into practice. By using **Scratch**, a free online coding software, we can start to actually build some live interactive code that can be tested and shared.

Scratch is a fun learning tool made specifically to help introduce coding principles. While it does not use a specific programming language as used by industry professionals, it is a great place to quickly create animations, games, quizzes, apps, and more, and will be an ideal starting point for beginner coders.

The Scratch workspace

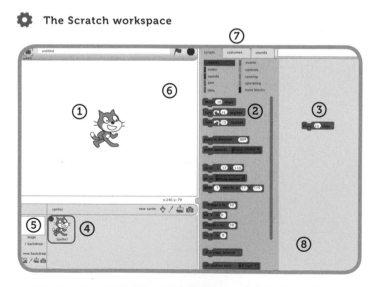

⚙ Elements of the Scratch workspace

Scratch lets you animate characters with easy-to-read coding blocks. The image on the opposite page is the standard interface for using Scratch, also known as the Project Editor screen. The software works by dragging code blocks into the "Scripts" panel, where they snap together to build programs.

(1) This is the **stage** where you can preview and test your project.

(2) The block palette contains all the potential instruction blocks. The tabs at the top all contain their own unique sets of blocks.

(3) The "Scripts" panel is where we add the code for our project. Simply click on one of the instructions from the block palette to the left, and drag it here.

(4) The sprite list shows each sprite used in your program. When you click on a sprite, its code will appear in the "Scripts" panel. New **sprites** can be added by clicking the icons at the top right of the sprite list panel (see page 60 for more details).

(5) Backdrops can be added from the backdrop library, hand-drawn, or uploaded from your computer. When you click on a backdrop, its code will appear in the "Scripts" panel.

(6) These icons will start and stop your program. The green flag means start running, and the red stop sign means stop.

(7) From left to right these icons can duplicate, delete, grow, or shrink your sprites. The final icon will help you troubleshoot.

(8) Drag and drop costumes, sprites, sounds, and scripts from projects into your "Backpack" to store them for quick and easy reuse.

▷ GETTING STARTED WITH SCRATCH

Scratch was designed with kids and teachers in mind, which is why it's available for from online. To use at home, you will need to have a computer with an Internet connection. The software is completely free, but will require an email address to sign up (see page 58).

SETTING UP SCRATCH

Creating your Scratch account and getting started with your first program is simple!

To begin using Scratch, visit the Scratch website at **scratch.mit.edu**

You will need to type this into your browser address bar, or alternatively use a search engine to look for "scratch software." Once on the Scratch homepage you will see a menu bar at the top with some options. You can click "Create" to go straight into building a project, but ideally should start by clicking "Join Scratch" so that you can save your work to revisit later.

SIGNING UP

You will first be asked for a username and password, which you will use in future to sign in. Remember to save your details or write them down somewhere safe in case you forget!

Afterwards, you will be asked for some details about your age and country, and then for an email address. The email address will be used in case you forget your password and cannot log in to Scratch, so you should make sure it is a real address you can access. You may receive an email from Scratch asking you to confirm your account, this way you can ensure you entered the correct email during sign-up and you should follow the instructions to confirm your email.

Following this, you should be signed up and ready to go, click the "Create" option in the top left to open up the workspace.

A BIT OF SCRATCH HISTORY

Scratch was created by the Lifelong Kindergarten Group at MIT in 2007 with the goal of making the principles of coding both intuitive and accessible for children all over the world. Scratch's motto is "imagine, program, share."

Though originally aimed at children ages 8–16, Scratch can be introduced to younger children with parental guidance, older children, and even adults who are getting started with coding. At an advanced level, Scratch can be used to create complex animations and games.

Scratch is used in more than 150 countries around the world, and is available in more than 40 languages. Click the globe at the top left of the Project Editor home screen to change the language.

 INTERNET SAFETY

Parents, if you are setting up a Scratch account for your children to learn and practice on, you should supervise them to begin with, and be mindful of Internet security.

 SCRATCH RESOURCES

There is lots to discover in the public areas of the site—you can browse projects created by others, as well as forums for sharing ideas and getting feedback. There are also guides and tutorials that can help you learn and grow your Scratch skills. We will focus on building new projects, but it would be helpful to explore the rest of Scratch yourself.

WORKING WITH SPRITES

Sprites are the visual elements that can be added to the "stage." They can be selected from a library of icons, or uploaded.

Scratch is used primarily for building and animating visual scenes, so imagery is important. In Scratch, every image, drawing, or background can be coded to move, change, or respond to an action, so they are all given the name "**sprites**." The term can also refer to frames in a game or animation in other software systems. When you start a new Scratch project there is already a sprite added—the Scratch cat on center stage! You can remove the cat (simply right-click and select "delete") or use it to experiment with some instructions.

 Sprite types

There are many different sprites to choose from, whether you want to use a pre-existing illustration, or create or upload your own.

 SCRATCH LIBRARY

Photos, cartoons, and drawings can be chosen from the Scratch library. Simply select one and add it to the stage.

 UPLOADS

Upload photos or images from your computer to personalize your sprites.

 DRAWINGS

Draw your own custom objects and characters for a truly original project. You can also draw over the existing sprites to edit them.

 BACKGROUNDS

Try adding a themed backdrop to enhance your stage designs.

⚙ Working with sprites

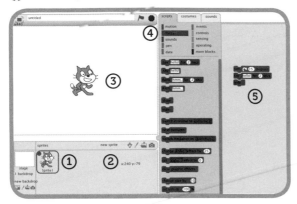

① This is where we can view our sprites and switch between them. The highlighted sprite in this panel is the one you are currently working on. Click a different sprite to select it.

② Here we can add new sprites to our project.

③ The sprites can be dragged directly onto the stage to begin working with.

④ These tabs will update to reflect the scripts, costumes, and sounds associated with the selected sprite. (For example, the Scratch cat comes with a meow sound, which isn't available to other sprites.)

⑤ The code visible in the script panel all refers to the selected sprite. Click a different sprite to see its code here.

▷ THE FRIENDLY FACE OF CODING

Scratch is one of the best places for kids to start coding—many schools are including it in curriculum as early as kindergarten! Parents, you can help get your kids get excited by picking out sprites that they will love— with a library of more than 250, they're sure to find a favorite!

INSTRUCTION BLOCKS

Instruction blocks are pieces of code that fit together to instruct sprites to change and respond.

It's finally time to begin coding. In the first chapter we looked at functions, which are lists of ordered instructions that tell a computer what to do. In Scratch, these instructions are called "instruction blocks," and are shown as colored rectangles that can be dragged and dropped into the "**Scripts**" area, where they will affect the selected sprite.

⚙ Using instruction blocks

With a sprite selected **(1)** and visible on the stage **(2)**, drag the blue "move 10 steps" block onto the "Scripts" area on the right. Now click on the block. You may notice your sprite will jump a little to the right. That's because you instructed the sprite to move by 10 **pixels**. Pixels are small, so try changing the 10 to 100 and clicking the block again. Now the sprite should make a big jump to the right. Try changing the number to -100 and click the block, you should see the sprite jump to the left.

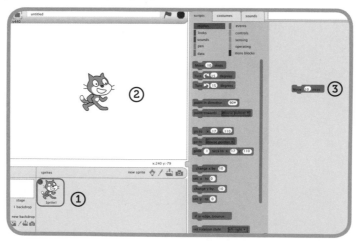

COMBINING BLOCKS

One of the great features of Scratch is the visual interpretation of code. The instruction blocks are made in distinct shapes, which snap together. A series of connected blocks is called a script. Sprites will always perform the script in the order in which the blocks are stacked.

 Experimenting with blocks

Now let's add more instructions to our cat: drag the block labelled "turn 15 degrees" underneath your "move" block. It should snap onto the first block and lock the two together, meaning your code now gives two instructions. Click on the code to test, and the sprite should complete the instructions to move and rotate in one movement.

Experiment with the instruction blocks by trying out a few combinations. For now, stick to the "Motion," "Looks," and "Sound" tabs as these will be easiest to see working right away. And remember that changing the input values will result in different outcomes.

 "Motion" blocks

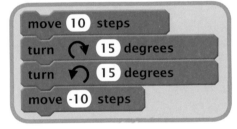

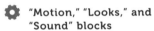 **"Motion," "Looks," and "Sound" blocks**

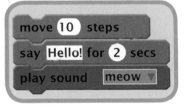

BLOCK TYPES

There are different types of instruction blocks filed under the "Scripts" panel at the top of the block palette. Within "Scripts," there are ten different categories of blocks. Blocks in the "Motion" tab all affect the sprite's position. Blocks found in the "Looks" tab change the visual appearance of the sprite, updating its color and size, or making it speak or think using bubbles with text. The "Sound" tab provides options to play sounds. These three types of code can be used interchangeably, and thus the blocks are all the same shape.

INTERACTIVE CONTENT

To make a program engaging for users, create code that can respond to "Events."

In the last section we made a sprite respond to some simple code instructions, but we want to make projects that other people can use and play. In Scratch, we can use "**Events**" to make our code run not just when we want it to, but when the user does a specific thing. "Events" blocks are essential tools for building interactive content, allowing users to click or type to make things happen, and they are also a common requirement in building websites or games.

USING EVENT BLOCKS

"Events" blocks are stored in the "Events" tab in the "Scripts" menu of the blocks palette. Most of them begin with "when...," so the subsequent script will be enacted when the specified event occurs. "Events" blocks have a rounded top wedge: this indicates that they cannot be added underneath another instruction—an event is always the start of any instruction set.

⚙ **When this sprite clicked**
Let's try out an "Events" block. Select your sprite, then click the "when this sprite clicked" block and drag it into the "Scripts" area. Next click the "Looks" tab and add the block "say [Hello!] for 2 secs" underneath. Now every time you click the sprite it will say "Hello!"—the sprite is now interactive.

when this sprite clicked

Keyboard Orchestra

Create this quick test project to see the benefits of interactive events and how they can be used to make projects engaging. We will be using the "when key pressed" instruction block, which will make the code attached run when you press the defined key on your keyboard. This allows you to run multiple instruction sets at the same time by pressing different keys.

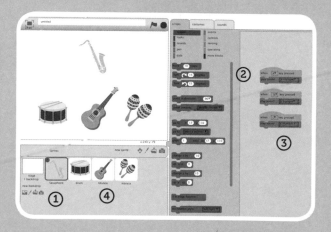

Directions for creating a Keyboard Orchestra

① Add a musical instrument sprite to the stage.

② Select the "when key pressed" instruction block and add it to your sprite's scripts. Define a key and then add the "play sound" block from the "Sound" tab (there should be a default musical sound selected, or you can choose from the list of sounds available to your sprite). In the diagram, you'll see we have used the "a" key and selected the sound "A sax," to go with the saxophone sprite selected. Try pressing the key to see if the instrument plays a sound!

③ Once you have a working instrument, try adding a few more notes or sounds to it. You can press the keys in a different order to compose your own tunes.

④ Try adding more instruments and playing them all.

ANIMATIONS

Using the "start" and "stop" buttons with "Events" blocks allows us to make video animation projects.

So far we have only made code that enacts precise instructions when specifically asked, but now we are going to create an animation that can run without the user needing to do anything. Scratch is ideal for building animations as you can easily move and edit the characters, and control the time that each animation takes to complete.

The green flag and red circle above the stage are the "start" and "stop" buttons for Scratch projects, and are a little like the buttons you might see on a video player. To make a sprite begin working when the green flag is clicked, find the matching instruction block in the "Events" tab.

 Aquarium animation

First, delete the cat sprite, and add a fish from the sprite library. Add an aquarium backdrop from the backdrop library. Add the "Motion" blocks below to your fish with the event block "when flag clicked" at the top.

Click the flag to run your animation: the fish should move and tilt a little. That's OK, but there are a few problems here:

1. The fish jumps and doesn't move smoothly.

2. The animation finishes very quickly.

3. We are repeating the same instructions over and over— remember our **DRY** concept from Chapter 1? (See page 38.) So let's improve this a little!

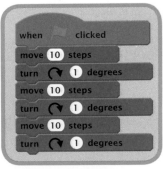

⚙ Improving our animation

The reason the fish jumps in one leap rather than moving slowly is because all the move steps are done very quickly. We need to add some pauses to create a motion effect. After each "move 10 steps" block, add a "wait 0.1 secs" block from the "Control" tab. This will make the code pause briefly before moving to the next step.

The fish should move a little better, but still only a short distance. We could add the same steps a few more times, but we do not want to repeat ourselves unnecessarily. Look for the "forever" block in the "Control" tab, which has a strange mouth-like shape. If you wrap this around any code it will continue to run the code over and over, meaning we don't have to repeat it ourselves. Attach this to the instructions and test again.

Success! Your fish swims smoothly, but it will quickly swim off the edge of your stage and be lost. To resolve this, add the "if on edge, bounce" block from the "Motion" tab, which will keep the fish on the stage.

⚙ Finished project: Aquarium animation

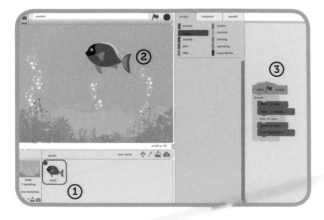

① The fish sprite is selected, so the code in the "Scripts" panel applies to it.

② The fish will swim around the screen indefinitely now!

③ The final code for our Aquarium animation.

VARIABLES

Create variables to store more complex information and allow your sprites to perform more advanced actions.

In the first chapter we looked at **variables**, and how they are used in coding to store temporary values that can be altered (like a score in a game). In Scratch, you can easily create and add "variable blocks" that can interact with your code, which are fantastic for building intelligent games. To emphasize this concept, we are going to make a search-and-find game using a score variable.

ADDING A VARIABLE

To begin, delete the cat and add the room backdrop and a bug sprite to the stage. Click the "Data" tab and select "make a variable." We want to make a variable called "score" which will keep track of how many bugs are found. After adding the variable, you will see that new instruction blocks are created for you to use relating to your new variable.

Add your bug to the stage and shrink it so it's harder to find (use the "shrink" icon in the menu bar at the top of the screen to quickly change the size of a sprite). Then add the following code:

1. When this sprite clicked

2. Change "score" by 1

This code will alter your variable by adding 1, so the score will add 1 whenever you click on the bug. The variable value should display in the top left corner of your stage, so click the bug to test that the number changes. We only want users to be able to click each bug once, so add an additional block from the "Looks" tab, "hide," so that once the bug has been clicked, it will disappear from the stage.

RESETTING YOUR PROJECT

Even when clicking the green flag to begin your game, Scratch will always begin from the previous setup, so if your bug is hidden, it will also begin the game hidden. We want the game to start the same each time so we can play again and again, so we need to add some reset instructions.

With the bug selected, add an additional instruction block so that when the green flag is clicked, the bug will show, this way your bug will always be showing when the game starts. We also want the score to start from zero each time, so with the backdrop selected, add this code:

1. When flag clicked   **2.** Set "score" to 0

Test your game again by clicking the green flag. You should be able to click the bug and your score increases, but it should then go back to 0 each time you start again. Using the "duplicate" icon from the menu bar at the top of the screen, select the bug to replicate the sprite and then move the duplicate to another position on the stage. The duplicated sprite will have the same code, meaning there are now two bugs to find, and clicking them both will take your score to 2.

Add more bugs to make the game more complex.

IMPROVING YOUR GAME

This is a great game to show to kids—it's simple to build, and perfectly playable after very little work. Next, let the kids come up with ways to improve it. There are lots of things that could be better! You could add more duplicate bugs (could you fit 100?) or add some new sprites, make sprites that are smaller and harder to find, or add a sound to be played when you click on a sprite so users know they have found something. What else can you come up with?

USER INPUT

Record user inputs as variables to customize the user experience.

In the last section we added number variables or **integers**, but our variables can also be **text values** or **strings**. We used our integer to increment a score, but we might use text variables to record text entered by the user. In Scratch, a sprite can ask for input, which can then be used in the project as a variable. **Inputs** are a common requirement in coding, most commonly used for making website forms and applications.

STORING A VALUE

In this sample project, we will use input instructions and variables to record inputs and make a sprite conversational. Select a sprite, then click the "Sensing" tab and add the "ask [What's your name?] and wait" instruction block to your scripts. Add the "Event" block "when flag clicked" to the top, then click the flag to test your project. You should see the sprite asking your name and an input box at the bottom of the stage. You can type in the box to enter your name, but currently we aren't saving the value, so the sprite will forget whatever you tell it!

We want a variable to save our name, so create a new variable (see page 68) called "name" then add these instructions to the script:

1. Set "name" to answer (from the "Sensing" tab)

2. Say [hello] name for 2 secs (start with "Say [Hello!] for 2 secs" from the "Looks" tab, and then see the diagram at the top of page 71).

This code will store our typed input as the string variable "name," and remember it.

⚙️ Storing an input variable

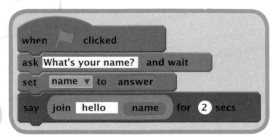

Adding the last block is a bit tricky as it involves adding the "say [Hello!] for 2 secs" block, then adding the green "join" block from the "Operators" menu, and "name" from your variables menu to create a compound command.

ANALYZING INPUT

As well as storing input values then repeating them, we can also use our variables to make different responses. We combined our string variable (name) with other text to give a response, but we can also **output** the length of the text (number of letters) or a specific letter **index** (such as the third letter). You'll see these options in the "Operators" menu.

Let's ask our sprite to analyze some data for us:

1. Ask [How old are you?] and wait

2. Set "age" to answer

3. Say (join [I'm 2 years old, so the age gap between us is] age – [2])

You will need to add a new variable called "age" and assign this to the response from your new question. The last command involves four separate blocks: "say [Hello!]," "join [hello][world]," "__-__," and "age," plus the keyed in values: "I'm 2 years old, so the age gap between us is" and "2."

The code asks the user for their age then does a sum to work out the age difference between the user input and the sprite.

⚙️ Final script

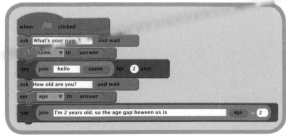

DYNAMIC FUNCTIONS

Add conditional flow to your project to prepare for different potential outcomes.

Our Scratch projects are now becoming more interesting. Using code instructions we can make characters move and talk, and even respond to user inputs, but they still do the same thing every time. In this section, we will look at adding **dynamic** control instructions, which can vary the instructions depending on the input. (Remember **conditional flow** from page 24?)

MATCHING YOUR ANSWER

In this project, we will make our character ask a question, then change the backdrop depending on the response. First, select "new backdrop," then add the "bedroom," "woods," and "city" backdrops. Next, select a sprite and add the following code:

1. When flag clicked

2. Switch backdrop to "bedroom 2"

3. Ask [Should we go to the city or woods?] and wait

4. If (answer = [woods] then)

5. Switch backdrop to "woods"

6. Say [Here we are!]

7. Else [blank]

With this code, we first set the backdrop (so it always restarts in the sprite's bedroom) then ask the question. We are then using the "if/else" block from the "Control" tab, which has multiple parentheses. This block will run different instructions based on the input given, and we have set it so that if your answer is woods, the backdrop will switch to the woods and complete the animation.

THE ALTERNATIVES

Test your code by answering "woods"—it should successfully take your sprite to the woods. But run it again and type "city"—nothing happens! This is because your "if" statement has not met the condition (answer = "woods") and so tries to run the "else" instruction, which is still blank.

We could put the instruction in here to visit the city, but then it would always go to the city when the answer is not "woods." Remember from the first chapter that we should provide a response for all outcomes, so instead we should add a second "if/else" block inside of our else instruction.

Add the following under your existing code:

1. If (answer = [city] then)

2. Switch backdrop to "city"

3. Say [Here we are!]

4. Else

5. Say [We will stay here]

By adding this additional block, we can provide a different instruction for three different outcomes; if the user requests "woods," "city," or neither. In the instance that the user does not select the city or woods the character will stay put and inform the user they have not selected either. Click the green flag to run the project and try each possible outcome.

⚙ Final script

HELPFUL METHODS

Use these extra tips and techniques to improve your projects!

AXIS VALUES

Placing sprites at specific positions on the stage is easy using axis values, and using them in your code gives you greater control over character animation. Every point on the stage has a specific x and y value, making up its vertical and horizontal position. The center point is 0,0 and moving left or down makes minus values and moving right and up makes positive values. You can see the axis values at any time in the corner of the stage by hovering on the stage with your cursor. The axis value for each sprite appears at the top right of the scripts panel.

RANDOMIZING INPUT

In our projects so far we have given specific values of how far to move or change a sprite, but you can add some variety to your projects by instead specifying a random number. Using the "pick random" block from the "Operators" tab, you can provide a range and make your sprite move, change size, or repeat tasks by random amounts every time your code runs (see script below). This can be great for making games more difficult and unpredictable.

⚙ **Random movement**

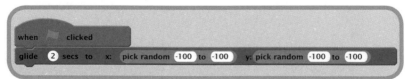

COLLISION DETECTION

Another valuable tool in Scratch for building games is the collision sensor. Using the "touching [___]" block under the "Sensing" tab, you can make instructions for what to do when a sprite touches another sprite or the cursor. These settings need to

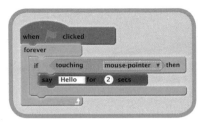

be wrapped in a "forever" loop (under the "Control" tab) to work properly, so the detection is constantly being checked and recorded.

PEN TOOL

Scratch has a whole tab of instruction blocks relating to its "pen" tool, which can be great for creating artwork in Scratch. The pen tool lets you draw with your sprite as if it were pushing a pen to the stage, and uses its movement to draw shapes with different widths and colors. There are many potential uses for the pen tool, including tracking your sprite's movement to debug an unexpected outcome.

COMMENTS

Remember our section in Chapter 1 about keeping code clean and easy to read? In Scratch, you can right-click on any instruction block and select "add comment" to add a little note about what the code does. This will not affect the functionality, but might be a useful way to keep track of which sections of the code are doing what.

You can also drag helpful code blocks to the "Backpack" on the bottom of the "Scripts" panel, which saves them for reuse elsewhere.

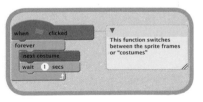

COMMON SCRATCH ISSUES

If your code isn't quite right, it could be one of these common issues. If you have further questions, take advantage of the Scratch Wiki. On your home screen, there is a "help" tab which will direct you to further resources.

 My sprite is becoming huge/tiny!

Remember that each time you run your code, the sprite will continue from its current position, so if your code makes the sprite bigger or smaller, it will keep changing each time without resetting to normal. For this reason you may need to add a reset instruction to your code such as "set size to 100%" at the beginning of your code. Now your sprite will reset to its usual size each time.

 My sprite isn't doing anything

This could be a number of things, but two common issues are no "Event" setting or wrong sprite selected. If you are seeing no response when you click the green flag, check you have set your code to run when the green flag is clicked. Check also the sprite that is selected in the library, as each sprite has its own "Scripts" area and you may be instructing the wrong sprite!

Not all of my code is running

It could be that your code blocks are not all connected, check they are joined and not just near each other. If only part of your code is running, it could be that you are using a conditional block such as an "if/else" block and so part of your code is being ignored.

 My variable says NaN

This means "not a number" and means you are trying to perform a mathematical function on a string value. If your variable is "Hello" and you try to add 1, it will be confused and return **NaN**. Consider what you are asking and reassign your variables appropriate values.

 My code just jumps and doesn't animate

This was a problem we faced in our animation section on pages 66–67: the code runs all your instructions so quickly that you don't get to see it smoothly animate. To fix this, use the "wait" block in the "Control" tab, and combine it with a repeated instruction to create a slower, visible animation.

 My sprite has vanished off the stage

Again, you might need a reset to put the sprite into a fixed point to start, using a block like "go to x(0) y(0)."

SCRATCH PROJECT 1: SCRATCH PARTY!

Now we know the basics, let's have a party to celebrate all the things we have learned in Scratch!

Test your knowledge by building this musical animation project! It uses many of the techniques you have learned throughout this chapter to create a simple party scene, which you can then add onto.

GET THE PARTY STARTED

Begin by adding the "party room" backdrop to a new project. First we'll need some music: click the "Sounds" panel above the "Scripts" area and select the "new sound" button. We are using the "dance magic" tune from the Scratch library, but you could add any tune or even upload your own song. Now let's set the scene with some lighting! You'll find the "change [color] effect by [25]" block in the "Looks" tab.

 Music

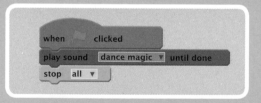

 Lights

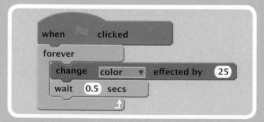

WHERE ARE THE GUESTS?

Our party needs some characters to complete the animation. If you still have the cat sprite on the stage, select it and add a setting to change costume and wait 0.5 seconds in a forever loop. This should make the cat dance and move while the music plays. Save this instruction block in your "Backpack" area at the bottom of the "Scripts" area and then apply it to some new sprites.

⚙ **Costumes**

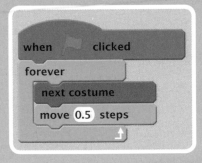

WHAT NEXT?

Here are some ideas for enhancing the "Scratch Party." What else can you think of?

- Try altering the wait and color change values to see what difference it makes to the scene.
- Edit your sprites' design in the "Costumes" panel to change their movements.

- Add the "singer" sprite, and place her next to the microphone. Can you come up with some code so that when clicked she begins to sing?

SCRATCH PROJECT 2: CATCH THE BUTTERFLY

Build this game then add a score to challenge your friends.

In this project, we want to return to using variables and control flow to build an interactive game. Follow the guide to get set up the game and then customize the settings to perfect and improve it. In this game, a butterfly will move randomly around the stage while you try to click on it. To begin, add a clear backdrop (we have used "blue sky") to a new project, then delete the cat and add a butterfly sprite to the stage. We want this game to have a time limit, so will need a variable to keep track of the time and tell us when the game ends, so add a new variable called "time."

SETTING THE TIMER

We want the time to begin at a specific number, then to tick down to 0 before stopping. Add the following code to achieve this:

1. When flag clicked

2. Set time to [20]

3. Forever {

4. If (time > [0]) then {

5. Wait [0.5] secs

6. Change time by [-1]

7. }

8. }

Take a look at the code to understand the function and how it works. The time is being changed by -1, meaning it decreases by 1 every 0.5 seconds, in a "forever" loop. The number would carry on going down forever, but an "if" block checks to see if the time is above 0. When the time reaches 0 it will stop counting down. Click the flag and watch the time variable on the stage, it should count down from 20 to 0 then stop.

THE FLYING BUTTERFLY

It's very easy to play the game so far, as the butterfly doesn't move! Add the following block into your loop to make the butterfly dance and fly around the stage:

1. Glide [0.3] secs to x: (random [-240] to [240]) y: (random [-180] to [180])

This simple line of code will run every 0.5 seconds inside our countdown loop and tells the butterfly to move around the stage. Rather than specifying a fixed point (which would be too predictable), we have used the random range block, and set it to the entire stage axis. Test the code: the butterfly will keep moving to new places and will be tricky to catch!

KEEPING SCORE

To make the game more fun, It would be good to know how many times you clicked on the butterfly during the game. For this we need to add a score. Add a variable called "score," then set it to increase by 1 every time you click on the butterfly. Add a check that the time is more than 0, too, so that you cannot keep clicking on the butterfly after the time has run out. Remember to reset the score to 0 when the game begins as well.

WHAT NEXT?

Here are some other ideas for improving this game:

- Change the values in the code to make the game harder or easier, such as speeding up the butterfly.
- Add another character that also moves on the stage. You could make it move faster and award more points for clicking on it.

- Add a sound that plays when you click the butterfly so users know they have increased their score.
- Set the butterfly to announce your score at the end of the game using a "say" block.

CREATE YOUR OWN SCRATCH PROJECT

Time to use what you have learned to build a brand new project!

While this book is a great guide, the best way to actually learn coding is by doing. The point at which you stop following a step-by-step tutorial and begin to think creatively about how to solve problems is when you begin to develop your coding knowledge, face challenges, and cement your understanding of coding topics.

Before moving on from Scratch, try designing and building your own project. Here are some ideas of things you could try.

RACE CAR

We have mainly used the "Event" blocks "when flag clicked" and "when sprite clicked" for our projects, but there is also great value in tracking when keys are pressed. Setting values on the up, down, left, and right arrow keys would enable you to move an item in different directions, such as a running, jumping character or racing car in a game. You could devise a track or course and set obstacles that when touched damage your car, or special booster objects that speed you up when touched.

THE BIG QUIZ

We looked at user inputs and variables in previous sections, but this idea could be developed further to make a full quiz application, increasing the user's score based on the answers they give. You can write your own questions then test with your friends. Remember to always plan for every possible input and save the inputs correctly.

PAINT SOFTWARE

We have not used the pen tool in any projects, but that is no reason not to experiment with this cool feature. Using the "mouse down" block, you could make a program that lets users draw their own designs on the stage. Once you have it working, you can give options to let users change the pen color and thickness. Remember to reset the stage whenever a new project is started.

REVISIT OUR PROJECTS

Remember, your projects are all saved in your Scratch account, so you can always access the existing projects we built in previous sections. If there was one you really enjoyed, you could go back and edit it, or even try rebuilding it in a new way. Keeping projects separate is helpful if you need to remember how you did something previously, and means you can revisit old projects to see how much you have learned.

 ASK FOR HELP

The opportunity to be creative makes Scratch a great tool for kids and adults alike. Parents, once you have worked through this section, you should have the basic understanding necessary to help guide kids through any trouble. And if you get stuck, there's always the Scratch wiki!

https://wiki.scratch.mit.edu/wiki/Scratch_Wiki

SUMMARY

What coding skills have we learned from Scratch?

In this chapter we have put our coding skills into practice by learning to build a variety of code creations in Scratch. The Scratch software is designed to be a great introduction to coding, and has enabled us to work with concepts such as variables, inputs, and conditional flow. Scratch is a great learning tool, but in the next chapter we will begin to use some "real-world" languages and use raw code. Rather than jumping straight into a functional language, we will learn about **markup language** and see how code differs from Scratch instruction blocks by learning HTML.

 REMEMBER

- Scratch is an online tool that lets you save and edit mini tools, games, and animations online.
- Variables are a fantastic tool for storing and analyzing information or user inputs.
- Remember to reset your projects to avoid unexpected appearance or function changes.
- Use the random range option to make sprites move or change in unpredictable ways.
- Scratch is a great environment for experimenting and a safe place to make mistakes.

5 TIPS FOR YOUR CODING PROJECTS

(1) **Scale up:** We have built our projects gradually by working in stages, as this is a good method for keeping your projects easy to test as you build. Instead of adding many sprites and making many "ifs" and loops, use one sprite and check each aspect works before gradually scaling up.

(2) **Sketch out a plan:** It's a good strategy to have an idea of what you want to build before you start. It's fine to change your mind or alter your composition, but not considering how you plan to make your project work could result in adding lots of unnecessary code, poor implementations, and errors. Make notes on what variables you need or what inputs are required to give you a clear focus.

(3) **Don't get stuck:** If you are spending a long time trying to make something work but getting nowhere, it might be a good idea to move on. Getting stuck will make you frustrated and bored, which will stop you learning. Take a break and come back to it later, you may find that a solution becomes clear while you are working on something else.

(4) **Borrow ideas:** The Scratch community is all about sharing projects and ideas, so take advantage of the things others have built. Click the "Explore" tab in the main menu to see other people's creations. See anything you like and you can open it to view the code that makes it work: a great way to pick up tricks and get inspired.

(5) **Share your work:** As well as looking at others' projects, feel free to share your own. Publish them online so others can comment and give feedback, but also share them with friends. Encouraging feedback will inspire you to build and improve projects and become a better coder.

WHAT ARE HTML AND CSS?

HTML stands for "hypertext markup language," and is used to write content for web pages. CSS is used to style web pages and is explained further on page 100.

Having grasped a great deal of coding concepts and philosophies, let's try some real hand-typed code, beginning with this chapter on **HTML** and **CSS**. These are not actually programming languages, so will not enable you to write functional instructions like we have done before. Instead, these will produce visual content to create websites. We will build upon coding concepts in the next chapter with **JavaScript**, but learning HTML will give you new skills to create web content and enforce some good coding habits. It's also a great way to get used to seeing and working with raw code.

⚙ Interpreting HTML

A web browser, such as Google Chrome or Safari, reads HTML and translates it into visual output.

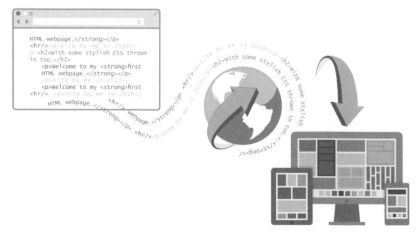

HTML IN ACTION

HTML is a **markup language**, meaning it uses blocks of information to format into a web browser. Unlike in **Scratch** where we simply add sprites to the stage, in HTML we construct our content with HTML **tag** blocks, allowing us to add text, images, forms, video, and interactive content. This chapter will cover the basic rules for working with these tags and show you some of the fantastic things you can do with them.

 HTML text and browser display

```
The word <strong>strong</strong> is bold.
```

The word **strong** is bold.

MINI-TASK: GET A FIRST LOOK

Open up a web browser and navigate to your favorite website. Right click on a space on the page and select "view source" (sometimes "show source," "view page source," or similar, depending on the browser). This will open up a separate tab showing you the code for that web page. This is the HTML that makes up that web page—you are looking behind the scenes to see what the page is made up of. We will be learning to write code just like this and build our own web pages.

GETTING SET UP

Set up an environment to begin creating web pages in HTML.

Over the course of this chapter, we will work in stages to build a web page in HTML and CSS. To follow the guide, simply add the required code where instructed and in the order presented. The theme of our page will be about the fun of coding, but if you want to change the text, colors, or any other details then feel free to customize the site to any topic you'd like.

You will not need an Internet connection to build the project, as we will be working **locally** (meaning the files are stored on your computer). You will need a web browser and HTML editor software, both of which you may already have on your computer or can download for free from the Internet.

HTML EDITORS

An HTML editor allows us to write our code in HTML files. You can use a simple text editor like Notepad or TextEdit, but a specific editing tool such as Sublime Text, Notepad++, or Adobe Brackets will be easier to use because it highlights and indents the code for you. Avoid any "WYSIWYG" (what you see is what you get) editors that let you create visually, or any "rich text" editors such as Word, as these will not save and render your HTML correctly.

WEB BROWSERS

A web browser (such as Google Chrome, Internet Explorer, or Safari) will render your HTML files visually and is needed to test your progress. You will probably already have one on your computer and while the display may differ slightly between them, you should be able to complete this project on any browser.

SET UP YOUR SITE

Create a new folder on your computer and call it "my HTML project." Add it somewhere that you will remember easily, like your desktop. Now, open your chosen text editor and create a new file, save it in your new folder as "index.html"—this will be our web page. Remember to add the .html to the file name. This sets the **file type** and your page will not work without it!

VIEW YOUR PAGE

Now open your new HTML file in your browser. If it doesn't open in your browser by default you may need to right click and select "open with" then select your browser. The page will be an empty white screen, as we haven't added any content yet. By keeping your file open in both your text editor and your browser, you can add some content, save your file, then refresh your browser to see how the changes look. You will have to repeat this process to test that your code is working as expected.

TEAM PROJECT

Parents, if your kids are learning HTML, then working through this project together will be great for both of you.

FOR REFERENCE

A full listing of the code for this project is shown on pages 124–127. If you become lost or your code is not working, you can use this as a guide to compare with.

HTML TAGS

HTML is constructed from content wrapped in blocks called tags. Let's add our first HTML tags!

HTML was first created in the early days of the Internet, and was originally intended mainly for text document use. Today, it is used for a wide range of content, but maintains its structure using HTML **tags**. An HTML tag is wrapped in less than (<) and greater than (>) symbols, contains a tag name, and usually features an opening and closing element. See below for a clearer example.

<h1>Hello world</h1>

OPENING TAG   CONTENT   CLOSING TAG

MINI TASK

Open your index.html file and simply write "Hello World." Save the file and then open it in your browser. You should see the plain, unformatted text. Now go back and change your text to this:

```
<h1>Hello World!</h1>
```

Save your file and refresh your page in the browser. The browser has interpreted your content as an <h1> or "heading" tag, and formatted the text as large, bold text. You just created your first HTML content!

ASPECTS OF TAGS

Types

There are many different types of HTML tag to do different things, for example:

<p> specifies normal (or paragraph) text
<u> specifies underlined text

Opening tag

Must use the less than/greater than symbols (< >) and contain a type (see above), this one uses <h1> for "heading text."

Closing tag

The closing tag is essential and only differs from the opening tag in the forward slash. This tells the browser to close the tag.

Content

A tag's content refers to anything contained between the opening and closing tags.

Nesting

Tags can be put inside other tags, but must be balanced, so they do not overlap (imagine using multiple sets of parentheses (in a very long (and likely ungrammatical) sentence))...

BUILDING AN
HTML WEB PAGE

Over the course of this chapter, we will build a working web page using HTML and CSS.

In the last section, we looked at HTML structure and added our first tags, but we have yet to set our page up properly. An HTML document contains two main sections: a **head** and a **body**. The head is for any code that is not directly visible on the page, such as settings, **styles**, and whatever needs to load before the rest of the page. The body is for the code content, such as our text and images.

We have learned that HTML tags have opening and closing tags, but it is important to note they are often nested or included within each other. For example, a button tag might be included inside a form tag, which is included inside a <div> or "division" tag, and all the visual content is included within the main body tag. The entire page content is included in one master HTML tag that defines where the page starts and ends.

START CODING YOUR WEBSITE

Delete any content on your index.html file and replace with this code:

```
<!DOCTYPE html>
<html>
<head>
    <title>My HTML Web page!</title>
</head>
<body>
    <h1>Welcome to my html page!</h1>
</body>
</html>
```

ANALYZING THE ELEMENTS

Let's take a look at the code we have just added in a bit more detail:

<!DOCTYPE html>

The first line sets the version of HTML for your browser to use. This setting is needed and will make sure our features work as expected.

<html> </html>

This tag wraps all of our content. The opening tag is the first tag at the top of our page, and the closing tag is the last line on our page.

<head> </head>

This area will be for the settings on our page. It currently contains just the page title setting.

<title>My HTML Web page!</title>

This tag sets the page title that displays above the page in the browser tab. Note how the content is written between open and closing tags—anything outside the tag is not included.

<body> </body>

This will eventually contain all of the page content, but for now it's just a heading tag.

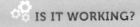 **IS IT WORKING?**

Save your file with this new code, and again open in your browser (or refresh the page if already open). Despite all the code we added, it should not look too different from before. You should see the heading (from the <h1> tag we added) and now the title should be visible in the tab, but the rest of our tags were just adding structure. We can now add more content to build and style our page.

MORE TAGS

Now we can begin adding more heading tags, text, and structure content types to our page.

We can now start adding text sections to set up our page using some new tags. We have added an <h1> tag to our page, which is a heading tag (traditionally used to title a page). An <h2> tag is also a type of title tag, which makes a slightly smaller heading, and there are also <h3>, <h4>, <h5>, and <h6> tags to make additional subheadings. For adding standard text to a page, we might use a <p> tag for "paragraph text." Some tags are used to style content, such as a <strong> tag for making text bold and an <em> tag for making text italicized.

ADD MORE TAGS

Add the following code underneath the <h1> tags you added to your index. html file on the previous page:

```
    <h2>With some stylish CSS thrown in too...</h2>
    <p>Welcome to my <strong>first HTML web page.</strong></p>
<hr/>
    <p>Site by me</p>
```

Be careful not to accidentally delete your </body> tag, which should stay at the bottom of the page. Change "me" in the last p tag to your name, if you like. Save your code and refresh your page. You should see that the text in the headings is slightly larger (see opposite page).

LOOKING AT THE DETAILS

`<hr/>` tag

We have introduced a new type of tag here—the `<hr>` tag, which stands for "horizontal rule." It doesn't contain any text or alter the styling, but instead adds a new line where added. This tag is a type of self-closing tag, meaning it doesn't have an open and closing element. See how its structure is different from the other tags?

Nesting

We have nested a `<strong>` tag within a `<p>` tag, meaning only part of the text has been made bold. This is a great way to highlight certain words or lines, but we have to be sure the tags close in the right order.

Indentation

We have intentionally indented the tags in this example to emphasize the `<hr/>` tag. As mentioned in the Coding Concepts chapter, this is a great habit to help organize your page as it grows.

⚙ **Our page with more tags**

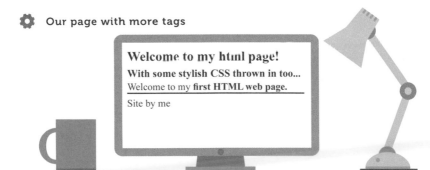

💡 MEMORIZING TAGS

Don't worry about trying to remember all these new tags. You just need to be able recognize them and see how they affect the way content displays on the page. You will quickly pick up tag names and formats if you are using them regularly, but it's fine to copy from existing code to save time.

SECTIONS AND DIVS

Add semantic elements to describe and structure your page.

We are going to adjust our page with some new tags to label and structure the sections of our project. Change the code listings where noted to update your page.

HEADER TAG

The <header> tag is an example of a semantic tag, meaning it describes the section of the page and makes it easier to understand what it does. Adjust your <h1> tag by wrapping it in the header tag like below:

```
<header>
    <h1>Welcome to my html page!</h1>
</header>
```

SECTION TAG

The next section of our page will be wrapped in a <section> tag, which is also a semantic tag, meaning a section of the page. Adjust the code after your header tag and before your <hr> tag with this code:

```
<section>
    <h2>With some stylish CSS thrown in too..</h2>
    <p>Welcome to my <strong>first HTML web page.</strong></p>
</section>
```

FOOTER

We have our header element, and now we are also adding a `<footer>` element, which is a tag for wrapping code on the bottom of your page. Replace your last `<p>` tag with this code:

```
<hr/>
<footer>
    <p>Site by me in 2016</p>
</footer>
```

We have wrapped our `<p>` tag in the footer, but also added an additional `<hr>` tag. This should mean you see two `<hr>` tags together, where we will add a new section later.

DIV TAGS

The `<div>` tag is for divisions of content on the page, and is extremely valuable for ordering and arranging the content on your page. It does not add any styling by default, but will be useful when we add styling later. Adjust your page by wrapping your body content inside a single `<div>` tag.

```
<body>
    <div>
        ...
    </div>
</body>
```

The "..." here represents the rest of the code so far added inside your body.

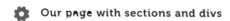 **Our page with sections and divs**

LINKS AND LISTS

Display information in interesting and interactive ways on your website with lists and link elements, and make your code clearer with comments.

LINKS

A common requirement is to add links so you can send users to helpful web pages or other sections of your website. Add this new links section between your two <hr> tags:

```
<section>
    <h2>Learning more coding</h2>
    <p>Here are some of my favorite links to other learning
    sites:</p>
    <a href="https://scratch.mit.edu/">Visit the Scratch
        website</a>
    <a href="http://www.w3schools.com/">W3Schools</a>
    <a href="https://www.bbc.co.uk/schools/0/computing/">BBC
    Schools - computing</a>
</section>
```

We have included a new <h2> and <p> tag, but also a collection of <a> tags, which are anchors or links. Links are used to make text that can be clicked, and link through to another web page.

The <a> tag requires an "href" **attribute**, which is added within the opening tag bracket. An "attribute" is a setting for the tag to provide additional detail; the href attribute tells a link where to go when clicked. Without this href element, the link will not work as it doesn't know where to go.

LISTS

Adjust your first section with the following code:

```
<section>
    <h2>With some stylish CSS thrown in too..</h2>
    <p>Welcome to my <strong>first HTML web page.</strong> So far,
    I have been learning about coding such as:</p>
    <ol>
        <li>A look at some coding concepts</li>
        <li>Building games in Scratch</li>
        <li>Designing web pages in HTML and CSS</li>
    </ol>
</section>
```

We have also introduced the <ol> tag, meaning "ordered list." The list tag is very helpful for menus and instructions, and must contain list items in an <li> tag. If you do not want the items numbered and only want bullet points, then change the <ol> to <ul>, for "unordered list."

LABEL YOUR CODE FOR CLARITY

We have discussed the importance of keeping code neat for you and others to read, and one way to do this is by adding comments to your code.
In HTML, there is a special structure to comment blocks so that the text inside does not get rendered on the page. Just add your comments inside of these tags: <!-- -->. For example, the <div> tag is not semantic, so we could easily get confused about what it does. Try adding the following code to make it clear that the <div> tag signifies the end of the page:

```
</div><!-- end of page -->
```

WHAT IS CSS?

CSS stands for Cascading Style Sheets and is a language for setting styling for web pages.

We have been learning about HTML by creating a well-structured web page using nested tags, but many of these tags haven't changed the way the page looks. This is because HTML is used for content, but for changing the appearance of our tags we need to use **CSS**.

CSS allows us to add color, fonts, spacing, and other settings to make our dry HTML look attractive. HTML and CSS work together to make websites, and as one is not much use without the other, we will learn how to add CSS to our page.

 Visual comparison of HTML and CSS

HTML	HTML with CSS
Structural Layer	Presentation Layer

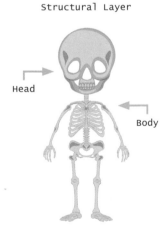

Head

Body

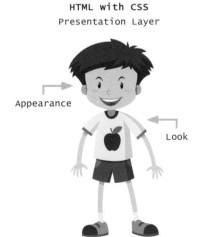

Appearance

Look

CSS STRUCTURE

The short piece of code below includes many key components of CSS:

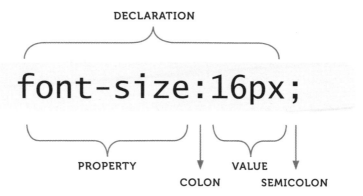

Declaration: This defines a visual change to be made and applies it to your web page. It is made up of a property and a value, separated by a colon

Property: This declares which setting to make. For example "font-size" sets the size of the text.

Colon: This separates the property and value.

Value: This defines the amount of the property, in this case, setting the font size to be 16 **pixels**.

Semicolon: Ends the CSS declaration, which means multiple declarations can be chained one after another.

EXAMPLES OF CSS PROPERTIES

There are many CSS settings, called properties, that can be used and combined to style your HTML. Here are some examples that we will be using in our project:

```
Background
Font-size
Color
Border
Font-family
```

ADDING INLINE CSS

Inline CSS is added directly to an HTML tag to change the styling.

We are now going to add some CSS to our HTML page to begin altering the design. We will begin with inline styling, which means adding the CSS **declaration** directly to an HTML element as a style attribute. An inline style setting will affect the tag it is applied to, plus any elements inside the tag.

Add this inline styling to your header tag:

```
<header style="text-align: center;">
    <h1>Welcome to my html page!</h1>
</header>
```

This inline setting will center your <h1> tag on the screen. Save your code and refresh your page in the browser—the <h1> text should now be in the middle of the page.

CHAINED DECLARATIONS

Add this styling to your <div> tag:

```
<div style="width:800px; border: 1px gold solid;">
```

We have made two declarations which are chained together and separated by a semicolon. The first sets the div area to 800 pixels wide, and the second sets a gold colored border of 1 pixel around it. Because our <div> tag contains all of our other content inside it, the entire page will be changed by this setting. Save your file and check your page in the browser.

Our links are all joined together on the page and should be on separate lines. Add the following inline settings to your links:

```
<a style="display: block;" href="https://scratch.mit.edu/">Visit
   the Scratch website</a>
<a style="display: block;" href="http://www.w3schools.
   com/">W3Schools</a>
<a style="display: block;" href="https://www.bbc.co.uk/schools/0/
   computing/">BBC Schools - computing</a>
```

By adding the display setting, we make our links into block elements, meaning that they display on different lines. Save the page and test this in your browser. With this edit we have added the exact same code three times, though this goes against our **DRY** (don't repeat yourself) philosophy. In the next section, we will make this simpler.

 Our page with inline CSS

Welcome to my html page!

With some stylish CSS thrown in too...

Welcome to my **first HTML web page.** So far, I have been learning about coding such as:

1. A look at some coding concepts
2. Building games in Scratch
3. Designing web pages in HTML and CSS

Learning more coding

Visit the Scratch website
W3Schools
BBC Schools - computing

Site by me

ADDING CSS STYLE BLOCKS

Target HTML elements by inserting CSS declarations directly into your page header.

When setting styles for our page, such as the color and size of text, we will often want many elements to have the same styles. Making many inline declarations would be a laborious duplication of code, so we will instead add a **style block** in our page's head, which lets us make one style setting for an entire HTML element.

CSS element declarations

```
div {
    width: 800px;
    border: 1px gold solid;
}
```

A CSS setting for an element is slightly different than adding an inline style. Instead of the style attribute, we define the element, then wrap all our CSS declarations inside curly braces { }.

This example shows how you would add a setting so that the text in all <div> tags would have a width and border setting. Rather than our current inline setting, which only works for the element we added it to, this would apply for any div element added to our page, so is much more efficient and avoids duplicating our code.

ADD A STYLE BLOCK

Adjust the head section of your index.html with the following code:

```
<head>
<title>My HTML web page!</title>
<style>
* {
    font-family: sans-serif;
}
div {
    width: 800px;
    border: 1px gold solid;
}
header {
    text-align: center;
}
a {
    color: CornFlowerBlue;
    display: block;
}
</style>
</head>
```

This adjusted header now includes a style block with some CSS settings for our page. The top setting with a "*" means this setting applies to all elements on the page, so we have made a font setting. There are also changes to our div, header, and tags—save, reopen the page and see how it looks in your browser.

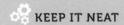 **KEEP IT NEAT**

Remember to remove all inline styles—we no longer need them as they are already set in the new style block. We will continue to add to this style area as we add elements to our page.

IMAGES

Add images to your HTML page with the <img> tag.

Most websites contain images such as logos, photographs, and illustrations. There are two steps to adding an image to a web page. Finding and saving the image, then adding the image tag to your HTML text.

ADDING YOUR IMAGE

Find the image that you would like to add to your page. An ideal image for this project is not too large (less than 800 pixels in height or width and under 200kb in file size). We are using an image called "dinosaur.png," but you can use any image that you already have, or download one from the Internet. Move your image to the same folder as your HTML file so that it can be referenced easily. Make sure your image name has no spaces, special characters (such as *-,%!), or capital letters, and is a simple, easy to recall label. For example, if your file is called "Dino Pic30659382.jpg" you should rename it to "dinopic.jpg."

⚙️ RENAME FOR SIMPLICITY

Moving forward, replace "dinosaur.png" in the code instructions with whatever you've chosen as your image name and file extension. It's fine to use .gif or .jpg files as well.

THE <IMG> TAG

Once your image is saved in the same folder as your index.html file, we can add it to the page using the <img> tag. Adjust your first section tag to include an image like this:

```
<section>
    <img src="dinosaur.png" alt="Dinosaur" />
    <h2>With some stylish CSS thrown in too...</h2>
```

The image tag contains two attributes:

- The "src" attribute defines which image to include and where to include it. Change your code to contain your image name followed by a dot and the **file type** (.jpg, .png, .gif, etc.). If your image is not displaying, it may be that you are misspelling your file name or using the wrong file type.

- The "alt" attribute describes your image. Change your code to include text that describes your image. This text will be displayed if the image isn't loading, or if the user has images disabled.

STYLE YOUR IMAGE

Save your file and test that the image is displaying in your browser. Next, we want to add some styling to change the way the image displays on the page, so add the following CSS into the style block in the page head:

```
img {
    max-width: 200px;
}
```

This setting means that regardless of the image's actual size, it will never display at larger than 200 pixels wide because it has a maximum width setting. Save and refresh your page. If your image was previously very large it will now have shrunk down. Note that this tag setting will apply to any images you add to the page.

CSS BACKGROUNDS

Set background colors, images, and gradients to improve your page display.

In this section, we will set up a background for our web page using the background property for the body, header, and footer. We will use named colors for most declarations, but in the footer, we will create a custom color using the RGBa setting, which lets us set the amount of red, green, and blue to combine. We will also add settings here for our <hr> tags so that they match our new colors. Adjust these properties, save your page, and test in the browser. It should start looking like a real web page now!

```
body {
    background: LightYellow;
}
header {
    background: gold;
    text-align: center;
}
hr {
        border: none;
        height: 1px;
        background: gold;
}
footer {
        background: rgba(255, 215, 0, 0.25);
        border-radius: 30px;
}
```

COLOR PROPERTY ELEMENTS

We have used the background property to change the background color of an element, but this can be defined in a few ways:

- **Named colors** are specific shades recognized by all modern browsers. Search "CSS color names" for more examples—there are 140 recognized color names.

- **HEX values** are letter number codes for specific color shades, prefixed by a # symbol. For example, #000 is black, #fff is white, and #FF7F50 makes an orange shade.
- **RGB values** set a specific color by combining red, green, and blue values. Some design software will allow you to see the RGB values of a color for use in web design. The fourth number given in the code refers to the colors' opacity.

BACKGROUND IMAGES

We can also set background images for our elements, which is sometimes helpful. This involves specifying the image to use and some optional settings for if the image should repeat or show once:

```
background:url("house.jpg") no-repeat;
```

This declaration will set the image "house.jpg" as the element's background, and the additional setting means it will only show once and not repeat.

BACKGROUND GRADIENT

We can also set gradients in CSS to create a smooth blend of multiple colors over the background.

```
background: linear-gradient(red, yellow);
```

This example will make the background a blend between red and yellow.

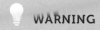 **WARNING**

Gradient effects may not work in all browsers as they are a modern feature. You may also need to add browser prefixes, which are browser-specific versions of this code. Search online for "CSS gradients" for examples.

SPACING WITH CSS

Adjust the position and gaps between objects with CSS padding, margin, and float.

Now that our page is bright and colorful, we just need a few more settings to make it display more evenly. In this section we will look at three property types for changing the spacing of the elements and their position on the page: the padding, margin, and float properties. Adjust your CSS with this new code:

```
div {
    width: 800px;
    margin: auto;
    padding: 0 30px 10px 30px;
    border: 1px gold solid;
}
header {
    background: gold;
    text-align: center;
    padding: 5px;
    margin: 10px 0 10px 0;
}
img {
    max-width: 200px;
    float:right;
}
ol li {
    padding: 5px;
}
a {
    color: CornFlowerBlue;
    margin-bottom: 5px;
    display: block;
}
footer {
    background: rgba(255, 215, 0, 0.25);
    padding: 10px;
    border-radius: 30px;
}
```

We have changed some of our elements to add padding and margins as well as adding a float property to our image. We have also added a new setting for our <ol> and <li> tags, which will affect our list items.

PADDING

Padding is used to increase the size of an element by adding extra space inside it. This means the text or images inside the element will have a wider spacing around them by the amount of pixels specified. In this case, our header and footer elements are now bigger because of the padding that has been added.

MARGIN

A margin adds extra space outside of the element, pushing elements away from it by the amount specified. You can set between one and four separate values (like we have done with the header), or you can specify just one side. The "margin: auto" setting on our div will even out the space on the page and center the element, regardless of the screen width.

FLOAT

The float property will make an element float to the side specified alongside the other elements. Our setting to the <img> tag means our image now sits on the right hand side of our text section.

 Before and after spacing amends

Before	After

STYLING TEXT WITH CSS

Style your text font, color, and size with these CSS settings.

We can further customize the design of our page by adding tailored changes to the text in CSS. We want to make changes to our headings and paragraph text, so adjust your CSS with these new settings:

```
* {
        font-family: sans-serif;
        font-size: 16px;
}
h1, h2 {
        font-family: monospace;
}
h1 {
        font-size: 3em;
        color: white;
}
h2 {
        color: lightseagreen;
        font-size: 2em;
}
footer p {
    font-size: 0.6em;
    margin: 0;
}
```

We have made two new types of declaration with this change. First, we have made a setting to both the <h1> and <h2> tags at the same time by comma-separating them, this helps prevent making duplicate settings. Second, we have added a setting at the bottom to specifically target <p> tags inside the footer, meaning those settings will not to apply to any other <p> tags. This lets us be more precise in our styling.

CSS FONT PROPERTIES

Font-size

We have used two different types of unit to specify font size in our CSS, pixels, and "ems." The pixel setting in the first element sets a default setting for our text (where not specified) to be 16 pixels high. Using ems, we can make our font size a percentage of that default size, so 1 em will be equal to 16 pixels, 0.5 ems will be 8 pixels, and 2 ems will be equal to 32 pixels.

Color

Similarly to background colors, you can set a named color, hex value, or RGB setting. We have added colors to make our headings stand out.

Font-family

To change the font of your text, use the font-family setting. The page will only render fonts which are installed on your computer, so to ensure everyone sees the same design try to stick to common fonts like Arial, Helvetica, Verdana, and Times New Roman. Custom fonts can be embedded into your page, which we will look at in a later section.

More font settings

There are many other CSS properties to style your text. If you want an effect but don't see it here, try searching online—it almost certainly exists!

text-transform:	Specifies UPPERCASE or lowercase
font-style:	Specify normal, *italic*, oblique
text-decoration:	Add <u>underline</u>, overline, or ~~strikethrough~~
letter spacing:	Set number of pixels between letters

IDS, CLASSES, AND PSEUDO STATES

Developing our CSS with targeted settings for classes and IDs, and the states of elements.

In the last section, we added a declaration to specifically target the <p> tags within the footer (with footer p {...}), but what if we want the same element to be styled differently in different instances? For this, we can use **CSS classes**, which let us set specific styling settings to any element. We can also set styling on the state of an element—changing the elements' styling when certain things happen to it. For example, when you hover over it and click.

Make the following changes to your code. First, change your div setting to an **ID** called "main":

```
#main {
    width: 800px;
    margin: auto;
    padding: 0 30px 10px 30px;
    border: 1px gold solid;
}
```

Then, create a new class called "themed":

```
.themed {
    color: darkorchid;
}
```

Finally, add a **pseudo** setting for your <a> tag hover state:

```
a:hover {
    font-size: 1.5em;
    text-decoration: none;
}
```

In the HTML body, change your <div> tag to include the main ID:

```
<div id="main">
```

Change your second <h2> tag to include the new "themed" class:

```
<h2 class="themed">Learning more coding</h2>
```

IDS

An **ID** is a unique identifiable part of the page, and allows us to make settings specific to that element. As we have one <div> tag that wraps our entire page, this is an important tag and should have its settings added to a main id to signify its importance. Now, if we add another <div> to the page, it will not inherit all the same settings, as it does not have an ID. You should only give an element one ID, and never use the same ID in multiple places.

CLASS

A **class** is a setting which can be applied to any HTML element for easy use. If, for example, you are commonly changing the color of many elements to red, it might be more efficient to create a "red-text" class with the red color property, then apply it to all elements you want to change. We have added our "themed" class to only one of the <h2> elements, so only this tag will inherit the style change.

PSEUDO CSS

We also added a setting for our <a> tag to increase the font size when hovered over. Save your file and refresh in the browser. When you move your cursor over the links they should increase in size because of this setting. This is called a **pseudo state**, and applies only to the tag in a certain state. You can also apply a setting for when an element is clicked (using :active) or to show it has been clicked before (using :visited).

CSS ANIMATIONS

Animate elements on your page with CSS animation settings.

CSS is not primarily an animation tool like Scratch; it was originally developed just for simple text styling. However, in recent years the progressive improvements in CSS and web browsers have meant HTML elements can be animated. While CSS is probably not the ideal tool for building many interactive moving elements, a well placed animation or two can make your web pages more interesting and eye-catching.

CSS TRANSITIONS

Add the following addition to your <a> tag CSS setting:

```
a {
    color: CornFlowerBlue;
    margin-bottom: 5px;
    display: block;
    transition:all 0.5s;
}
```

Save your file and refresh your browser. We have added a setting to make text larger when hovered over. This new transition setting will give the effect of the text growing in size (this will happen over 0.5 seconds). Setting "all" will make any changes animate if they have a numerical setting like "font-size" or an RGB color setting.

KEY FRAME ANIMATIONS

To make a full animation, we need to set the animation **parameters** using key frames. In the bottom of your CSS style block, add this code:

```
@keyframes dance {
    from {transform: rotate(0deg);}
    to {transform: rotate(25deg);}
}
```

This code will create an animation called "dance," which sets an element to rotate 25 degrees clockwise. This format has a simple "from" and "to" definition, but you can also create more complex animations using percentages. Search "CSS animations" online for different **syntax** examples.

We now need to add this animation to a class so we can use it in our page. Create the new class "animate-this" with the following code:

```
.animate-this {
animation-name: dance;
    animation-duration: 4s;
    animation-iteration-count: infinite;
    animation-direction: alternate;
}
```

As well as setting the animation, we have also set some additional options for how the animation should work. We have set the animation to last four seconds, repeat infinitely, and run forward then backward. In our last code change, we will add our new "animate-this" class to our image so it will inherit the properties and animate:

```
<img class="animate-this" src="dinosaur.png" alt="Dinosaur" />
```

Test your code by saving and refreshing your page. Your image should now gently tilt on repeat with its new class.

💡 **WARNING**

CSS transitions and animations may not work in all browsers, and could need browser specific prefixes to work in all instances. If your animation is not working, try opening the page in a different browser.

RESPONSIVE HTML/CSS

Adapt your web page to different screen sizes with responsive CSS settings.

One of the challenges for modern web designers is the wide variety of online devices that may be used to visit their web pages. From a small cell phone to a wide-screen monitor, the different sizes create difficulty in providing a web page that effectively uses the available screen space. For this reason, modern CSS now features **media queries**, which allow you to create CSS settings specific to the screen width or height. This allows your website's design to respond to any screen size, and is called **responsive design**.

ADD A MEDIA QUERY

First, we need to add a "viewport" tag to our page head. Place this line below your title tag before the style block:

```
<meta name="viewport" content="width=device-width,
initial-scale=1.0">
```

⚙ TESTING YOUR PAGE

Your page is still offline as it is saved locally, so you will not be able to test that it is working on a mobile device. However, if you save and refresh your browser, you should be able to drag the corner of your browser window to resize the browser width. When the browser is less than 800 pixels wide, the page should alter to display an adapted display.

Then, add this code to the bottom of your CSS style block:

```css
@media (max-width: 800px) {
    * {
        font-size: 12px;
    }
    #main {
        max-width: 100%;
        padding: 0;
        border: none;
    }
    img {
        float: none;
        max-width: 100%;
    }
}
```

Media query elements

A media query has a specific syntax, let's take a look in more detail.

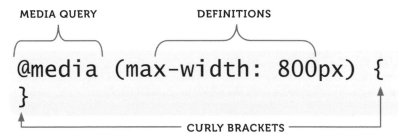

- We define a media query with @media

- The definitions are in parentheses: this CSS will only apply if the screen size is under 800 pixels wide. You could additionally add minimum screen widths, heights, or even settings for print.

- The CSS is then added within curly braces {} and added as regular CSS. This will overwrite the settings already applied to those elements.

We have added three new settings for smaller screen widths. First, we have reduced our base font size, meaning all our font sizes set with ems will be reduced on smaller screens. Second, we have removed margins and widths for our containing div: by using percentages instead of pixels it will always fill the full width of it's browser. Finally, we removed our image float and set a "max-width" property so it will fill the screen on it's own line.

USING EXTERNAL LIBRARIES

Harness the power of external scripts and styles to add extra features to your websites.

We have hand-typed every single line of HTML and CSS code to build our web page so far, but you can sometimes get extra help to add features from other sites. By attaching external **scripts** and styles to your page, you will essentially connect your page to another online file so that you can use its features. This allows you to take advantage of extra perks that can improve the look and function of your site. Here we will add some custom fonts, icons, and embed a Scratch project using external scripts.

ADD CUSTOM WEB FONTS

As mentioned on pages 112-113, you can only add fonts that are installed on your system. With **web fonts**, however, you can attach a font just to the page—so you can use all kinds of custom fonts! We will use the Google Fonts library: go to fonts.google.com to look through available fonts.

When adding a font, you must add two pieces of code to connect it to your site. First, add the <link> tag (provided on the site) to access the font:

```
<link href="https://fonts.googleapis.com/css?family=Comfortaa"
rel="stylesheet">
```

This gives us the ability to use the "Comfortaa" web font. Then, apply the font where needed in the CSS. Adjust your headings setting to use the font with this CSS:

```
h1, h2 {
    font-family: "Comfortaa", cursive;
}
```

The heading tag and CSS will be different depending on the font chosen, but instructions and code are provided on the site. Our site should now use a custom web font.

ADD FONT ICONS

External fonts can also be used to give us icons. We will use the Font Awesome library. Rather than images, the site provides text rendered as images. To begin, visit fontawesome.io and select "get started." You will need to provide an email address to get your custom script file, which must then be added into the header, as per the example below:

```
<script src="https://use.fontawesome.com/123456789.js"></script>
```

Then, by selecting icons from the site, HTML code is provided to simply paste icons into your pages. Here we are adding an icon into our <h1> tag:

```
<h1><i class="fa fa-file-code-o" aria-hidden="true"></i> Welcome
to my html page!</h1>
```

EMBED A SCRATCH PROJECT

We can also import entire web pages and content into our site using **iframes**. Certain sites provide embed code for you to easily grab content such as videos and add it to your site. Scratch provides the embed code so that you can add entire projects into your web pages—look for the embed option on your project title page. Pasting the code into your page should then load a full Scratch project into the <iframe> tag.

 TROUBLESHOOTING

Sometimes, an external library may not load because your web page is not online, and so the site has not allowed the content to be shared. These features are something you may wish to revisit when publishing web pages online.

COMMON ISSUES

Some mistakes and errors often made when learning HTML.

Moving into real code can be a tricky adjustment. Here are some potential problems that may occur.

 I can't edit my content

It's important to remember that with HTML, it's all in the code. Tools like Scratch let you drag and drop content but with HTML it is read through, and gets output in the browser. If you are trying to edit text or move images in the browser nothing will change!

 My changes aren't showing on the browser

Have you saved your file and refreshed your browser? It needs to be done every time you make a change to see the newest version of your file. If simple changes like your text are not changing then it is probably one of these things.

My code isn't showing correctly on the screen

There are many things that could be wrong, but a good first step is to check your code for **formatting** errors.

- Have your closed all your tags? Remember, a closing tag has the / inside to denote ending, otherwise it will just read as another opening tag.

- Are your tags overlapped? Look at where tags open and close, if one is half inside another and the nesting is wrongly structured, it will confuse the browser and cause display errors.

- Typing edits? Are you using the right case for your tags? Are you adding/missing any spaces? Are your class names matching their name in the CSS? Simple typing mistakes will cause big problems.

 My images are not displaying

Again this could be a few things. Check your image is added to the same folder as your file, check you have spelt the name of the image correctly and that the file type matches. Note that a **JPEG** image has the file type written as image.**jpg**—which can be confusing.

 DEBUGGING YOUR PAGE

One of the tough things with HTML can be simple mistakes causing big problems with your display, but it is also one of its strengths. The visual display gives you clues about what is not working properly and changing values will give you feedback as to what is. Referring to our project code on pages 124-127 and comparing it with your own may be a helpful exercise. Remember that fixing problems is also a valuable coding skill.

FULL PROJECT CODE

```
<!DOCTYPE html>
<html>
<head>
<title>My HTML Web page!</title>
<meta name="viewport" content="width=device-width, initial-scale=1.0">
<script src="https://use.fontawesome.com/123456789.js"></script>
<link href="https://fonts.googleapis.com/css?family=Comfortaa" rel="stylesheet">
<style>
* {
    font-family: sans-serif;
    font-size: 16px;
}
body {
    background: LightYellow;
}
#main {
    width: 800px;
    margin: auto;
    padding: 0 30px 10px 30px;
    border: 1px gold solid;
}
header {
    background: gold;
    text-align: center;
    padding: 5px;
    margin: 10px 0 10px 0;
}
h1, h2 {
    font-family: "Comfortaa", cursive;
}
h1 {
    font-size: 3em;
    color: white;
}
h2 {
    color: lightseagreen;
    font-size: 2em;
}
.themed {
    color: darkorchid;
}
```

 CHECK YOUR WORK

The full code for the website you've been building throughout this chapter is displayed here for your reference.

```css
hr {
    border: none;
    height: 1px;
    background: gold;
}
img {
    max-width: 200px;
    float:right;
}
ol li {
    padding: 5px;
}
a {
    color: CornFlowerBlue;
    margin-bottom: 5px;
    display: block;
    transition:all 0.5s;
}
a:hover {
    font-size: 1.5em;
    text-decoration: none;
}
footer {
    background: rgba(255, 215, 0, 0.25);
    padding: 10px;
    border-radius: 30px;
}
footer p {
    font-size: 0.6em;
    margin: 0;
}
.animate-this {
    animation-name: dance;
    animation-duration: 4s;
    animation-iteration-count: infinite;
    animation-direction: alternate;
}
@keyframes dance {
    from {transform: rotate(0deg);}
    to {transform: rotate(25deg);}
}
@media (max-width: 800px) {
    * {
        font-size: 12px;
    }
    #main {
        max-width: 100%;
        padding: 0;
        border: none;
    }
    img {
        float: none;
```

```
            max-width: 100%;
        }
        iframe {
            width: 100%;
        }
    }
    </style>
    </head>
    <body>
    <div id="main">
        <header>
            <h1><i class="fa fa-file-code-o" aria-hidden="true"></i>
Welcome to my html page!</h1>
        </header>
        <section>
        <img class="animate-this" src="dinosaur.png" alt="Dinosaur" />
        <h2><i class="fa fa-paint-brush" aria-hidden="true"></i> With
        some stylish CSS thrown in too...</h2>
        <p>Welcome to my <strong>first HTML web page.</strong> So far,
        I have been learning about coding such as:</p>
        <ol>
            <li>A look at some coding concepts</li>
            <li>Building games in Scratch</li>
            <li>Designing web pages in HTML and CSS</li>
        </ol>
        </section>
    <hr/>

        <section>
        <h2 class="themed"><i class="fa fa-thumbs-up" aria-
        hidden="true"></i> Learning more coding</h2>
        <p>Here are some of my favorite links to other learning
        sites:</p>
        <a href="https://scratch.mit.edu/">Visit the Scratch website</
        a>
        <a href="http://www.w3schools.com/">W3Schools</a>
        <a href="https://www.bbc.co.uk/schools/0/computing/">BBC
        Schools - computing</a>

        </section>
    <iframe allowtransparency="true" width="485"
    height="402" src="http://scratch.mit.edu/projects/
    embed/123456789/?autostart=false" frameborder="0"
    allowfullscreen></iframe>
    <hr/>
        <footer>
            <p>Site by me</p>
        </footer>
    </div><!-- end of page -->
    </body>
    </html>
```

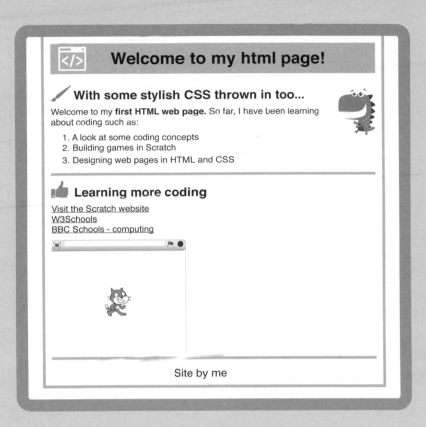

Welcome to my html page!

With some stylish CSS thrown in too...

Welcome to my **first HTML web page.** So far, I have been learning about coding such as:

1. A look at some coding concepts
2. Building games in Scratch
3. Designing web pages in HTML and CSS

Learning more coding

Visit the Scratch website
W3Schools
BBC Schools - computing

Site by me

BUILDING WEBSITES TOGETHER

Use these pages to help you to check and debug your web page as needed. Once you have seen how relatively simple it is to create a basic web page, work with your kids to create a personalized page about something you enjoy. This is also a great opportunity to talk to your kids about private versus public pages and Internet safety.

CODING CHALLENGE: CREATE YOUR OWN DESIGN

Build your own new web page from your own design and link it to our project.

We have taken a tour of HTML and CSS by building a web page and introducing its key features, but it is also important to learn by doing and creating. It can take a while to get used to the format and quirks of a language, and a helpful challenge to set yourself may be to build your own page with your own HTML elements and CSS styling. This will force you to re-read and analyze the code in this chapter and deepen your understanding, but will also give you the opportunity to practice fixing errors to produce working code.

CREATING A NEW PAGE

Create a new file in your HTML editor and save it in the same folder as your index file with the name "page2.html." The only required code for your page to work properly is the basic page setup shown on page 93, as these are essential tags for every web page, but the rest is up to you!

LINK TO YOUR FIRST PAGE

Looking to link your pages? Add the following code to create a link to the first page:

```
<a href="index.html">View my first HTML web page</a>
```

MAKE COPIES

If you are worried about losing work or breaking your page, make frequent copies at intervals. Simply right click your file and select the duplicate option, or copy and paste it. This works like saving your progress in a game: if you make too many mistakes in your file and cannot fix it, you can easily revert to your saved copy.

NEW PROJECT IDEAS

Project idea 1: Redesign your first page

Use your new skills to improve on the first page you built in this chapter. Add extra content and features or change the styling to a new design. Instead of starting afresh, it may be simpler to make a copy of your index.html page, but don't work directly over your original as you may want to refer back to it.

Project idea 2: Make a blog

Design a page for you to write about your code learning experience. This will need a central column with a heading, the date, and your text. Add photos, videos, and links to your post content, then write multiple posts on the page. Remember to add spacing to clearly separate each post.

Project idea 3: Make a comic strip

Use images and CSS to create a series of image panels and tell a story. You may need to use <div> tags to contain your image and text, plus some CSS to add padding and a border to each div. A float setting will make the div boxes sit next to each other in a line, plus a colored background will make the boxes stand out.

BOOTSTRAP

Use the Bootstrap CSS library to quickly scaffold your projects.

As we saw in the external libraries section on pages 120–121, attaching external scripts and libraries can quickly improve your web pages by introducing cool features, and this can extend to an entire CSS framework. **Bootstrap** is a CSS library that is used by many popular websites: it provides pre-built CSS code that lets you add pre-designed elements to your page so you can quickly set up professional-looking web pages. These elements can be adjusted with your own themes, but the baseline saves time and can also solve many compatibility issues that come from different browsers and devices.

SETTING UP

First, create a new HTML file using your text editor and save it to your folder. Add the standard website structure shown on page 93. Visit getbootstrap.com for the Bootstrap CSS website. From here select "getting started" from the menu, where advice is given for setting up Bootstrap. There is a block of code provided called a **CDN** (content delivery network), which means these files are hosted elsewhere so you do not need to download and add them to your own website directory (though you could also do that). Copy these and paste them in your new page's head. That's it—you are now set up to use Bootstrap components.

USING BOOTSTRAP

Go to "CSS" from the menu: here you will see a full documentation of things this library lets you add to your page. Adding a <div> with the "container" class will automatically add a centered block with padding for putting your content in, which will also adapt to smaller screen widths. You can also use the CSS 12-column grid setup, meaning you can get content to align in columns of different widths, which is a very valuable design tool. For example, the following code will create two equal width columns that align next to each other:

```
<div class="row">
    <div class="col-md-6">I am the left column</div>
    <div class="col-md-6">I am the right column</div>
</div>
```

Selecting the "components" tab from the menu, you will also see code examples for all kinds of useful HTML elements. Buttons, form elements, icons, menus, and labels can all be imported so that you won't have to spend a long time building everything.

WHAT'S BEST FOR YOU

It is important to realize these features are all built using the same HTML and CSS we have learned in this chapter, rather than any new technology. The main reason you may choose to use Bootstrap is for its quick installation, consistency, and shared support, but using a common library could make your website look similar to other websites.

As you are starting to learn HTML and CSS, Bootstrap can be a useful kick-start and a reference for tips, but it could also prove confusing. It may be easier to avoid it until you are more confident with your code.

PUBLISHING YOUR SITE ONLINE

A brief summary of web hosting and options to help you get your code online.

Your HTML files are stored locally on your computer where you can access them, but ultimately web pages are built for viewing online. To be accessible online, your files need to be stored on a server, which gives them a **remote** location that other Internet users can connect to in order to access the files. You are probably familiar with downloading files from the Internet, but pushing your page online is a form of uploading to your hosting location.

This creates two versions of your site: a local copy on your computer, and a remote copy online. Keeping both means that you can easily make any changes to your local version then push the updates to your live version.

⚙ Uploading to the Internet

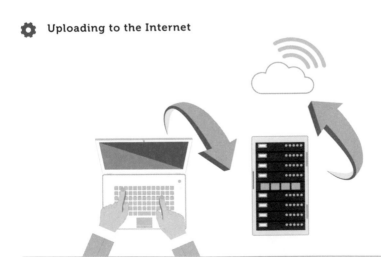

CODE REPOSITORIES

There are various resources for saving HTML code online and testing the display. Trinket (trinket.io) is a great resource for creating quick code snippets, with code highlighting and a visual display to test your code. Codepen (codepen.io) is a similar tool and also has a network of coding samples to help and inspire you, much like Scratch.

WEB HOSTING

There are many places that offer free online web hosting, and you can usually purchase hosting with a custom domain, which means that your pages can go to any web address you want (if available). You can either upload your files via the hosting control panel, or via an **FTP** (file transfer protocol) software.

There are also some services such as GitHub pages, which hosts GitHub code repositories as web pages. Search online for web hosting options and see what's right for you.

SAFETY FIRST

Before putting anything online, it is essential to discuss Internet safety with your kids. And remember, anything posted online can potentially exist forever, so upload only after careful consideration.

SUMMARY

What have we learned about HTML and CSS in this chapter and through building our first web page?

In this chapter, we have begun to set up a coding environment and use real code by learning HTML and CSS. We have also been able to put some coding principles into practice, such as presenting formatted code, debugging, and minimizing excessive code. In the next chapter, we will return to programming with JavaScript, a language that will also enable us to add behaviors, and give us greater interaction with our web pages.

 REMEMBER

- HTML is a markup language for creating web content.
- HTML is built with combinations of tags that a browser interprets to create web pages.
- CSS is used to style HTML elements with settings for position, color, and fonts.
- External resources can be attached in the head of your documents to allow extra tools and functionality.
- A web page needs to be uploaded to a remote hosting location to be accessible online.

5 TIPS FOR YOUR CODING PROJECTS

① **Use the inspector:** Most browsers contain a "dev tools" feature that gives developers access to various information for testing and debugging. Among the tools is an "inspector," which lets you select HTML tags on the page and see their CSS properties, which can be a great way to understand how your page is working.

② **Draw out a wireframe:** Jumping in without a plan can be fine when you're just getting started, but for more organized projects this can be the perfect recipe for errors. If building your own page, it might be best to sketch out a rough design and figure out which elements will be needed on the page to create it. Working to a plan is much easier.

③ **Search for help:** We have taken a very brief run through many HTML topics and only covered a selection of HTML tags and CSS properties. Following the code will help you create tags but searching online will be a valuable resource for extra detail and options to vary the content.

④ **Format your code for easy reading:** Code can be complex and hard to understand at the best of times, so make life easier for yourself by formatting the code in an easy to read structure. Put tags on new lines, add indents to nested tags, and add comments where needed—you will thank yourself when it's time to make edits.

⑤ **Open and close tags:** You may develop all kinds of quirks and habits as you begin to write code that help you work more efficiently and avoid mistakes. One tip that may help is remembering to write a closing tag straight after your opening tag and then adding your content in the middle, that way you will not forget to write it in at the end.

WHAT IS JAVASCRIPT?

JavaScript is a programming language for adding behavior to web pages.

In the last chapter we began using real code to build web content using **HTML** and **CSS**. In this chapter we will revisit some more coding concepts with the **JavaScript** programming language, which will then enable us to enhance our web pages.

HTML, CSS, and JavaScript are commonly learned together, as they can be combined to make well designed, functional web content. While HTML and CSS provide the content and styling, JavaScript adds the functionality to make your web pages interactive. JavaScript is widely used in the web development industry, requires no complex installation and has a wide range of interesting uses. Learning JavaScript will give you a chance to improve your code learning and habits, but will also be a valuable starting point for building your own coding projects.

 Elements of a web page

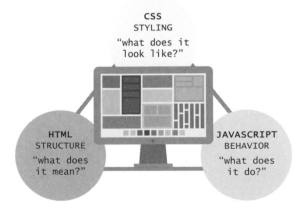

JAVASCRIPT VS SCRATCH?

JavaScript works similarly to Scratch and is also used for giving functional instructions to alter **output**. But while Scratch is focused on animating sprites on the stage, JavaScript is focussed on analyzing information to alter the behavior of a web page. The **syntax** and structure are different, but you may find comparisons and crossovers in their aims, and the familiarity you have gained with Scratch will help you learn JavaScript.

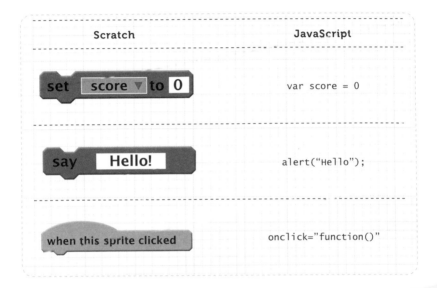

Scratch	JavaScript
set score to 0	var score = 0
say Hello!	alert("Hello");
when this sprite clicked	onclick="function()"

IN THIS CHAPTER, WE WILL COVER:

- **Variables, loops, and functions** in JavaScript
- **Responding** to user **events**
- Manipulating the browser **DOM** with JavaScript
- Saving data with the web storage **API**
- Simplify JavaScript using the **jQuery** library

MATH IN JAVASCRIPT

Begin by getting started with the browser console and familiarizing yourself with some simple sums and comparison logic.

We don't need any new software to begin learning JavaScript, simply create a new empty .html file in your text editor, then open it in your browser. We will be using the browser **console** (sometimes called the JavaScript console), which is part of your browser **developer tools**. In Google Chrome, you will find it in (View/Developer/JavaScript console), but this will differ depending on the browser you use, so search online for "how to open JavaScript console in ___."

WRITE A JAVASCRIPT COMMAND

The console is a place for logging messages and running JavaScript commands. Try typing this code into your console then hitting return:

```
alert("Hello")
```

Your browser should flash a new **alert modal** with a "Hello" message. If your alert did not work, check you added the apostrophes and parentheses in the correct order. You have just written your first JavaScript code!

⚙ **Alert modal**

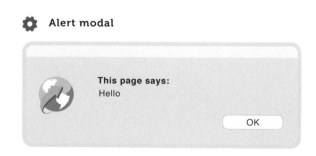

SIMPLE SUMS

JavaScript allows you to run mathematical sums, which can be combined to perform useful functions. Try running some simple equations in your console. Remember to press return to run the function.

The console should return the result of your sums underneath.

 Mathematical sums in console

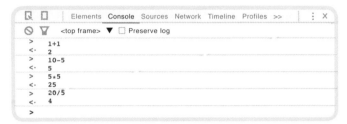

COMPARISONS

As well as simple mathematical queries, we can also use JavaScript to make the console compare values and return a **Boolean** value (true or false). Typing **1 == 1** into the console will return **true**, as we are asking if one is equal to one; typing **1 > 2** will return **false**, as one is not more than two. Try a few variations in the console using the comparison operators. These quick functions can be used for more than just numbers and are valuable tools in finding and checking information.

==	equal to
!=	not equal to
>	more than
<	less than

VARIABLES

Let's recap the concept of variables and learn to use them in JavaScript to save information.

In JavaScript, the information you query may be numerical, as in the previous examples, but will more commonly be a saved value that represents something important in your functions. As we learned in Chapter 1, this is called a **variable** (pages 30–35), which can be **strings**, **integers**, **Booleans**, or combinations of these in **arrays**. Variables allow us to save values temporarily, which can be altered, checked, and combined as part of a **function**.

Still using your browser console, let's revisit the first three variable types and how they can be used.

INTEGERS

Integers are whole numbers, which can be used for sums and comparison functions. This example sets an integer variable for a person's age.

Defining a variable in JavaScript, you must write **var** followed by the variable name, then define its value and end with a semicolon. This example has saved the term "age" to a value of 25, so that you can perform mathematical or comparison functions on the variable "age" like you would any other number:

```
var age = 25;
age + 10
➤ 35
age > 10
➤ true
```

BOOLEANS

Boolean values are simple true or false values, which can useful for checking something with just two states (such as a checkbox in a form).

They are key to functions' decision-making processes. You define a Boolean variable as you would an integer, only with a true or false setting:

```
var learnToCode = true;
learnToCode == true
  ➤ true
```

STRINGS

Strings are text values defined in the same way as integers and Booleans, but with one important difference: strings must be wrapped in quote marks to define where the string starts and ends. Strings can contain numbers, have spaces, and contain the words true or false, but will be treated as strings as long as they are defined correctly:

There are various methods that can be run on string variables, such as .length, which returns the number of characters in your string:

```
var firstName = "Michael";
firstName.length
  ➤ 7
```

They can also be combined with the mathematical + symbol, and as they are not numbers they will not be added together but joined:

```
var lastName = "Jackson";
firstName + lastName
  ➤ MichaelJackson
```

Try making your own variable types and combining them in the console. Variables only remember the last value they were set to, so try redefining a variable to a different value.

FUNNY FACT

Notice the example variable name used above, "learnToCode," has no spaces, as variable names need to be one word. The capitalization of each new word makes the variable easier to read and is called **camel-case**.

OUTPUTTING RESULTS

Learn to write your code in script files and output your results.

To begin writing more complex functions in JavaScript, we will need to save our code so that it can be altered and improved. As we have seen from these first tests writing variables in the console, JavaScript is native to the web browser and doesn't require any new software installations, so we just need to create a file to run in our browser.

SETTING UP FOR JAVASCRIPT DEVELOPMENT

Create a new HTML file with the editor software you used in the HTML chapter. Add the following HTML, which contains an empty web page structure with the addition of a <script> tag which will contain our JavaScript code. Save the file, then open in your browser, and open the developer console. The console should have a "Hello" message that it reads from your file.

```
<!DOCTYPE html>
<html>
    <head>
    </head>
    <body>

    <script>
        console.log("Hello");
    </script>
    </body>
</html>
```

DIFFERENT OUTPUT METHODS

Console log

In the setup code on the previous page, we added a **console.log** function with the value "Hello." This is a helpful function, which will print any value between the parentheses to the console when the page is loaded. This can include variables or the results of functions, and is commonly used in **debugging** to test the code output is working as expected and to help define a problem.

```
console.log("Hello");
```

Alert

Another output method is an **alert**, which will also load a value on the page when loaded, except in a warning box. Alerts are used to notify users in an obvious way, and the user must dismiss the box to continue, so they are ideal for critical errors or very important notices. An alert function has a similar structure to **console.log**, with the output value between parentheses. Try replacing the line **console.log("Hello");** in your text editor with an alert:

```
alert("Watch out!");
```

Confirm

A "confirm" function will also open a modal with a message, but gives the user two buttons: confirm and cancel. This way the user is faced with a choice, and their response will be a Boolean value you can use as part of a function.

```
confirm("Are you sure?");
```

Prompt

Finally, a "prompt" function will open your message in a modal box, but instead prompts the user to enter a message. The message can be saved as a variable, and could be used to get information from the user.

```
prompt("Please enter your name");
```

CONDITIONS

Use conditional flow in JavaScript to adjust your potential outputs.

In our statements so far we have compared two values to output a true or false response, such as equal to, more than, etc. In this next section, we will take our comparisons further with an output based on the response using **conditionals**. We have already gained experience with conditional flow in our Scratch chapter, and you will see many similarities with the JavaScript syntax.

IF/ELSE

We want to compare the age of three people in our code. Begin by creating three number variables in the <script> tag of your file, like this:

```
var matt = 12;
var hassan = 7;
var sarah = 15;
```

We can now compare the values using an **if/else** statement, which will respond differently depending on the outcome of our value comparison. Below is an if/else statement to compare the value of variable "matt" to see if it is more than variable "hassan." If it is, the console will let us know Matt is older, otherwise it will log the opposite statement provided in the else block.

```
if(matt > hassan) {
    console.log("matt is older");
}
else {
    console.log("hassan is older");
}
```

The if/else block statement contains the comparison in parentheses. Here is where we make the statement to be evaluated (if variable "matt" is greater than variable "hassan").

```
if(matt > hassan) {
    // Code to run if the expression is true!
}
```

Any code placed inside the curly braces will execute if the result is true, otherwise it will be ignored and code inside the "else" code braces will be run.

```
else {
    // Code to run if the expression is false!
}
```

ELSE IF

Should you need to check more than just two potential outcomes, you can also add an "else if" statement inside your conditions. You can add as many additional else if conditionals as needed after your first "if" statement.

In this example, we are checking that Sarah at least 10 years old and able to attend a class. We have also provided a response for if she is too young or if she is too old, so there will always be a response.

```
if(sarah < 10) {
    console.log("You are too young!");
}
else if(sarah == 10) {
    console.log("You are welcome");
}
else {
    console.log("You are too old!");
}
```

Try writing an if/else statement analyzing variables of your own, then save your file and open it in your browser. The console should only output one of the potential values.

ARRAYS

Arrays are JavaScript lists that are useful for storing collections of variables and data.

An array is most commonly used when you would like to perform an action that sorts or affects a group of variables, rather than just one. For example, in the last section we wrote some code to check a person's age, but if we want to do the same check for many people at once, we will need to use an array. An array is declared in the same way as other variables, but with square brackets containing the list of items.

SAMPLE ARRAYS

```javascript
var cats = ["Ginger", "Sooty", "Spots", "Cuddles"];
```

The variable above, named "cats," creates an array of cats. Note that the items in the list are string values, so are wrapped in quote marks, and also that each item is separated by a comma so that the code knows to keep them apart. An array can contain any combination of information types, including integers, Booleans, and even other variables. See below.

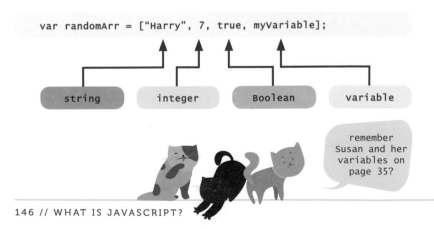

```javascript
var randomArr = ["Harry", 7, true, myVariable];
```

string   integer   Boolean   variable

remember Susan and her variables on page 35?

ARRAY METHODS

JavaScript has many types of inbuilt methods that allow users to sort, search, remove, and combine list items to build helpful functions.

For example, to add a new item to a list,, use the **.push** method:

```
var birds = ["Toucan", "Cardinal", "Parrot"];
birds.push("Pigeon");
birds = ["Toucan", "Cardinal", "Parrot", "Pigeon"];
```

We can now check the new bird has been added by checking the number of items in our list using the **.length** method:

```
birds.length
➤ 4
```

ZERO INDEXING

Each item in a list has an index, which is the order in which it appears (first, second, third, etc.), but in JavaScript, the index of the first item is zero. This means the index of the second item is one, the third is two and so on. This is important to remember, to avoid referencing the wrong item in a list by querying the wrong index.

```
var birds = ["Toucan", "Cardinal", "Parrot", "Pigeon"];
birds[1]
➤ "Cardinal"
```

"Cardinal" is the second item in the list, but has the index of one.

Check the index of an item using the **indexOf** method, as below: we can find the index of our fourth item ("Pigeon"), which is three:

```
birds.indexOf("Pigeon");
➤ 3
```

LOOPS

Learn to repeat code on multiple items using a JavaScript for looping.

One of the benefits of using arrays is that code can be executed on each item on a list. Using **loops** in a "**for-loop**" structure, we can specify a list of items and some instructions, and the code will run for each item in the list. A loop can reduce code replication, adhering to the **DRY** philosophy, but is also easier to maintain. Even when adding new items to a list, the for-loop will not need updating as it checks each item in the list, regardless of updates.

THE FOR-LOOP

Here is an example of a JavaScript for-loop, which will log a list of shopping items in a sentence:

```
var items = ["cheese", "milk", "eggs", "bread"];

for(var index = 0; index < items.length; index++) {
    console.log("I bought " + items[index] + " at the
    store");
}
```
```
➡ I bought cheese at the store
➡ I bought milk at the store
➡ I bought eggs at the store
➡ I bought bread at the store
```

ELEMENTS OF A FOR-LOOP

var index = 0;

We set a new "index" variable, which represents the iteration in our loop.

index <

Items.length; We set the number of times to loop, which we set to the length of our array

Index++

We set the index variable to increment and begin looping!

console.log("I bought " + items[index] + "at the store");

The method, or command, which is looped.

This code, combined, will repeat the instructions inside the curly braces. Inside our instructions, the "index" variable can be used to refer to the current iteration in our loop. For example, items[index] will refer to the first item in the list, then the second, third, and so on as the loop progresses.

PUTTING IT TOGETHER: FIND REX!

Using a for-loop on our array, we can then use an/if statement and comparison logic to build a smart function. This example will search our "dogs" array (below) and log to the console if the dog "Rex" is found in our list.

```javascript
var dogs = ["Spot", "Max", "Rex", "Fido"];
for (var index=0; index < dogs.length; index ++){
    if (dogs[index] == "Rex") {
        console.log("Rex is in the list!");
    }
}
```

Try writing this code in your script file and testing in the browser console, then try adapting the array values or code instructions. This search function is helpful, but needs to be manually changed if we want to search for a different dog, and we can only run this code once at a time. In the next sections, we will make our code more dynamic with defined functions and **parameter** options.

FUNCTIONS

JavaScript functions are reusable blocks of code designed to perform specific tasks.

This chapter has given us methods to interpret and analyze information using conditions, comparisons, and loops on variables, but we can still make our code more effective. Firstly, our code runs whenever we load the page, which we may not always want it to do. Secondly, it runs once, and if we wanted it to run multiple times we would need to copy the code, which is bad practice. To solve these issues, we will introduce named **functions** to save our code blocks.

A function is a saved piece of code that can be invoked or "called" when required, rather than by default. Functions help segment your code and make it easier to manage. They can be set to run instantly or, if given a name, can be run multiple times when called.

SAMPLE FUNCTION: MYFUNC

```
function myFunc() {
    console.log("function has been run");
}
```

This function is named "myFunc" and all the function will do is log a message to the console. If you run this code in your browser you will see nothing, as the function hasn't been called yet! To make it work, call the function with the following code:

```
myFunc();
```

We can also make the code run as many times as needed. Make the function run multiple times with the following code:

```
myFunc();
myFunc();
myFunc();
```

FUNCTION SYNTAX

Function structure has some new elements we have not seen before:

```
function myFunc()
```

After writing "function," we add the name of our function, which can be anything with no spaces. The parentheses following it are empty but could also contain parameters, which will be covered in the next section.

```
{ }
```

Then we write the instruction inside curly braces.

```
myFunc();
```

Using the function name, parentheses and semicolon will call your function, so long as it has been defined already.

THE RETURN

A function can undertake many types of task, but can also have a definitive ending and response. Using a return statement, the function will be stopped and the value is returned as the result of the function.

```
function myNewFunc() {
    if(5 > 4) {
        return true;
    }
    if(1 != 2) {
        return false;
    }
}
```

In this example, we have created two simple "if" statements using number comparisons. The first query (five is more than four) is correct, so the function will return true. The second query (one is less than two) is also correct, so the return would be false. Logging this function will test the result:

```
console.log(myNewFunc());
➡  true
```

The console output only logs true, meaning the second query was never run. This is because the return value completed the function, so all code below that line was ignored. The return statement is a valuable way of segmenting functions and providing clear endpoints in your code.

PARAMETERS

Parameters are options included within functions that enable each call to respond uniquely.

Using named functions we can save and reuse our code when needed, but the function will still provide the same response every time it runs. In order to make our code **dynamic** (meaning it will analyze different inputs and create a helpful "thinking" code), we need the ability to pass in different values.

Using function **parameters**, we allow the function to take optional input values and use them as part of the function logic. With parameters in your function, every time it is called you can pass in different **arguments** to affect the result.

PARAMETERS AND ARGUMENTS IN A FUNCTION

```
function sayHello(name) {
    console.log("Hello " + name + " , how are you?");
}

sayHello("Bill");
sayHello("Terry");
sayHello("Jim");
```

The function "sayHello" takes a name parameter, which it then uses to log a welcome message. We then call the function three times, each time providing a different name argument. These produce the following output:

```
➤ Hello Bill, how are you?
➤ Hello Terry, how are you?
➤ Hello Jim, how are you?
```

FUNCTION ELEMENTS

Adding parameters adapts the way we construct and call our functions:

function sayHello(name) { We name our parameters inside the function parentheses, which can be empty if no parameters are needed. We can add more than one, but must separate them with commas

console.log("Hello " + name + " , how are you?"); The parameter name can then be used as a variable in your function, but will only work inside your function code.

sayHello("Jim"); When we call the function, we provide a definition for what the parameter should be. The values passed into a function are called arguments.

ANALYZING PARAMETERS

We can use the parameter as an output value, but can also use it to determine which response is given. In this example, our code checks your age to see if you are old enough to see a film:

```
var allowedAge = 12;
function checkAge(age) {
    if (age < allowedAge) {
        return console.log("Not allowed");
    }
    else [
        return console.log("Allowed");
    }
}
```

The function **checkAge** takes a name parameter and then checks its value in an if/else statement. Depending on the parameter value, it will return a message allowing or not allowing the user to see the film. We have set our allowed age to a **config** variable rather than a number—this provides a simple way to adjust our function if needed. Running the function will now output different results each time.

```
checkAge(10);
➜  "Not allowed"
checkAge(5);
➜  "Not allowed"
checkAge(40);
➜  "Allowed"
```

USER EVENTS

Make your code respond to user events on the page.

JavaScript enables us to build smart functions and calculate information, but can also work with HTML page elements to respond to user behavior. Ultimately, we want users to provide values for our functions to interpret, rather than coding them ourselves each time, so we want to connect our code with user events on web pages.

ADDING A BUTTON

Using the empty page we created for our practice JavaScript code (see page 138), add an HTML button tag to the page with an **ID** of "myButton" in your page body:

```
<button id="myButton">Click me</button>
```

Then in the script block at the bottom of the page, add this code:

```
var button = document.getElementById("myButton");
```

This code attaches a new variable "button" to the button tag using the JavaScript **getElementById** method. This targets the item matching our chosen ID and allows us to access the tag in our code. We can now respond to our web page elements using JavaScript.

ONCLICK EVENTS

A user event means something completed by the user, such as hovering, clicking, dragging, or pressing a button. Having saved our button to the variable "button," we can now apply events and make our page respond when those events are triggered. In the following code, we attach a function to the onclick event, meaning the page will display a message when the button is clicked:

```
button.onclick = function() {
    alert("clicked");
};
```

Add this code and test it in your browser. You should get a page alert every time the button is clicked.

DYNAMIC RESPONSES

We can also apply the techniques covered in previous sections to make dynamic responses to user events. In the following code, we set a number variable, then make the number increment every time the button is clicked.

⚙ **Number variable**

This example demonstrates how user interactions can provide a new form of input for our functions to analyze, and is an essential tool for building games and applications.

```
var button = document.getElementById("myButton");

var myNum = 0;

button.onclick = function() {

    myNum++;

    alert("You clicked " + myNum + " times");

};
```

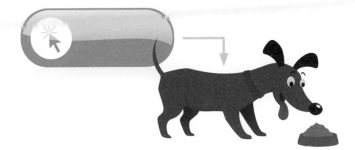

USER INPUT

Retrieve and handle user inputs with HTML and JavaScript.

In the last section we attached our code to HTML content so that it could respond to user events. In this section we will look at handling user input, which will allow us to analyze text values and receive dynamic inputs.

CREATE A PASSWORD

We want to build a page with a password field. Add the following HTML to your body to create the form:

```
<label>Password</label>
<input id="password" type="password" />
<button id="submit">Enter</button>
```

We have added a label and input tag for users to enter their password, plus a button to submit their attempt. The following code will read your input field input then log it to the console:

```
var button = document.getElementById("submit");
button.onclick = function() {
    var passAttempt = document.getElementById("password").value;
    console.log(passAttempt);
};
```

Try the code in your browser and see your password attempt written in the browser.

READING VALUES

The code in this example is adjusted from our first onclick function:

```
var passAttempt = document.getElementById("password").value;
```

We create a new variable (passAttempt) each time the button is clicked, and use the .value method to read the value entered into the input field. Saving the value to a variable allows us to read and analyze the input. Now we just need to hook up the password validation.

ANALYZING THE INPUTS

By adding an if/else statement to our function, we can decide if the user has entered the correct password. Adjust your code to the following then test in your browser:

```
var button = document.getElementById("myButton");
var correct = "codingisfun";
button.onclick = function() {
    var passAttempt = document.getElementById("password").value;
    if(passAttempt == correct) {
        return alert("You have entered the correct password");
    }
    else {
        return alert("That password is incorrect.");
    }
};
```

The correct password has been stored as a string variable: find it in the code and you will know how to match it and test your page. Checking a user's password and other form input is a very common requirement in websites. Additional complexity in the code may check that a value has been entered or a minimum number of characters are supplied.

HELPFUL METHODS

Try these additional tricks to help your JavaScript coding.

 Math.round

There are many number methods using the **Math** object that can help adjust numbers. This one will convert any decimals to round numbers.

```
Math.round(28.24);
➤ 28
```

 Math.random

Sometimes a random number can add variety to a game or application. By calling the **.random** method, it will generate a randomized decimal between 0 and 1, combining this with **Math.round**, you can generate one of two random values.

```
Math.random();
➤ 0.44075828324466926
```

 parseInt

Another helpful method is **parseInt**, which can convert a string value to a number, a great way of altering user inputs.

```
parseInt("15 years");
➤ 15
```

toLowerCase

When comparing string values from user inputs you may need to check both uppercase and lowercase letters, adding extra code. By using this method, you can convert your value to lowercase and check the value once.

```
toLowerCase("My dog is called Rex");
➡ "my dog is called rex"
```

substring

Need to trim your string values? Use the **substring** method to shorten its length. For this method you provide two values: the index to begin at and how many characters to trim to.

```
var name = "Christopher Smith";
name.substring(0, 5);
➡ "Chris"
```

Array join

If you no longer need an array to be a separated list, you can combine the items into a single string with the **join** method. A string can also be converted into an array using the **split** method.

```
var hobbies = ["Sports", "Cinema", "Reading", "Games"];
hobbies.join();
➡ "Sports,Cinema,Reading,Games"
```

Array splice

Need to take an item out of your array list? Using the **splice** method you can choose the index of the item to remove, how many to remove, and even extra values to replace those values.

```
var spices = ["Nutmeg", "Cinnamon", "Ginger", "Cumin"];
spices.splice(0, 1);
➡ ["Cinnamon", "Ginger", "Cumin"]
```

COMMON ISSUES

There is plenty of potential for your JavaScript development to accrue errors or not function correctly. Frustratingly, this is all part of the learning process, but here are some frequently made mistakes to watch out for, and their possible solutions.

 My output is picking the wrong element

This may be an issue with **zero indexing**, which we covered briefly on page 147. The first item in your array uses index 0, and so every subsequent item may be one less than you first expect. In a list of four items, there will be nothing for index 4, so If your function finds nothing, it may be referring to the wrong index.

 My number isn't incrementing

If your variable isn't working as expected, it could be the wrong variable type. If your variable is wrapped in quotes, such as "7," then it will be treated as a string regardless of content, and mathematical functions will not work. You can use a **typeof** operator to check which type of data you are using (**typeof "7"**), and there are even methods that will convert your data type.

My console reads "undefined"

Your console is not just great for outputting values and testing, it will also provide error messages to help you discover faulty code. If a variable is described in an error as undefined, it means you are referring to a variable that can't be found. You may be misspelling a variable: remember, they cannot contain spaces and are case sensitive, so "myvariable" is a different variable to "MyVariable." Check the order of your code too: are you analyzing a variable before it has been defined in the code?

 My code isn't outputting anything

This could mean many things, but could also be an error in the way you have structured your functions. In all our examples, we have tried to produce a result regardless of the outcome, does your "if" statement also have an "else"? A helpful way of discovering the issue could be by setting some additional **console.log** statements at different points in your code. See also the debugging advice on page 42.

 My page is breaking and crashing the browser!!

JavaScript is a fast loading language and should load very quickly, especially when you are not downloading your code from an external web page. If there is slow loading on your page or your browser crashing, it could be that a loop or function is repeating endlessly and making your page work too hard. For instance, calling a function inside the function itself means it will constantly be re-running, or a for-loop that will output values until 1 is more than 5 will of course run forever. Beware infinite loops for the obvious reason that they create fatal issues in your programs.

JAVASCRIPT PROJECT 1: SUPERHERO CREATOR!

Practice your skills by building a random superhero generator.

Coding is easiest to learn when you're inspired to build cool new projects. In this section, we will use JavaScript to build an application that creates superheroes, and can be adapted or developed in many ways. To create it, you will need an HTML file with script block in the body as we have created for other samples in this chapter.

GETTING STARTED

For our project structure, we will create a series of arrays containing sentence fragments. We can then select a random index from each and combine them in a new sentence. Finally, we will output the result in an alert, so a new hero will be created every time the page loads. To begin, create an array of adjectives containing a series of descriptive strings:

```
var adjectives = ["The fantastic", "The magnificent", "The
incredible", "The marvellous"];
```

Then, underneath, we create an array of names. Make sure it contains the same number of values:

```
var names = ["Avenger", "Captain Flame", "Phantom", "Ultra
Ninja"];
```

We also need a list of powers to complete the description, so create a third array of powers:

```
var powers = ["can walk through walls", "can travel through
time", "can summon lightning", "can breathe underwater"];
```

We now have the content to pick from and begin our functions.

PICK FROM YOUR LIST

We want a mini-function that will generate a random number for us to pick from our lists. Using the random and round number methods in combination, we will generate a number between 0 and 3, which is returned as the value when the function is called.

```
function getRandom() {
    var num = Math.round(Math.random() * 3);
    return num;
}
```

The function will return four possible values. Remember to adjust if you add any extra values to your arrays.

GENERATE THE HERO

To create the actual function, we create a hero variable, which combines one value from each array (separated by spaces), then alerts the result. Using our random function, we can select a new index from each array every time the function runs, meaning we will create new combinations of superhero types.

```
function generateHero() {
    var hero = adjectives[getRandom()] + " " +
names[getRandom()] + " " + powers[getRandom()];
    alert(hero);
}
```

Finally, we need to call our function:

```
generateHero();
```

This app could be adapted with more options, more elements to the character definition, or even a parameter for selecting from different arrays. Try creating and adapting to further understand how it works.

JAVASCRIPT PROJECT 2: WHAT'S THE TIP?

Take user inputs to make custom calculations in this mini-project.

In this mini-project, we will return to handling user input by building machine that calculates tips. Users can enter the cost of a meal, add their percentage tip, then get a breakdown of the costs. Create a separate HTML file for this project, again using a basic page setup with script block at the bottom of the body for your code.

GETTING STARTED

Begin by adding the following HTML in your page body:

```html
<div>
    <label>Enter the cost</label>
    <input id="cost" type="number" />
</div>
<div>
    <label>Whats the tip percentage?</label>
    <input id="tip" type="number" />
</div>
<button id="myButton">Enter</button>
```

This code contains two input fields, each with a separate ID so they can be accessed in our JavaScript code. We also have a button which will run the function.

GRAB THE VALUES

Now for the functional code. First, we attach our button to a variable so we can respond to the click event:

```
var button = document.getElementById("myButton");
```

Then, in our click function we get the values of our two input fields. Note that we are using the **parseInt** method to convert our inputs from strings to numbers.

```
button.onclick = function() {
    var cost = parseInt(document.getElementById("cost").
    value);
    var tip = parseInt(document.getElementById("tip").value);
};
```

Then, by dividing the first value by the second we will create a variable for the tip. We then use that variable to calculate the total cost. Finally, we output the result in an alert. The adjusted function is shown below.

```
button.onclick = function() {
    var cost = parseInt(document.getElementById("cost").
    value);
    var tip = parseInt(document.getElementById("tip").value);

    var result = cost / tip;
    var total = cost + result;
    alert("Tip will be " + result + ". Total cost: " + total);
};
```

Test the function to calculate a tip value. The application could also be adapted to take an additional value for the number of people to divide the bill amongst, or to add a sales tax.

ADJUSTING THE DOM

The browser DOM is the model of the web page that can be accessed and altered.

Through our examples and projects, we have learned how to read values from HTML tags and input using JavaScript. JavaScript is able to read information from the page but also push information onto the page, as it has access to the browser **DOM**. The DOM (Document Object Model) is a construction of the page and its elements that JavaScript uses to access and manipulate. This makes JavaScript a very powerful tool for web, as it allows complete control over content and making live changes to the page.

By accessing the browser DOM, we can

- Create HTML elements
- Move or adjust page elements
- Alter the styling and other **attributes** of page elements

- Make elements hide and show
- Change classes to alter appearance and animate page elements
- Change text content

 Document Object Model

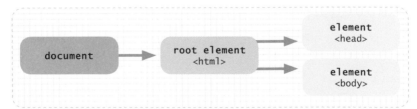

CREATE CONTENT WITH JAVASCRIPT

Let's build a simple example to demonstrate how a page can be updated with JavaScript. Build a simple HTML file like this:

```
<!doctype html>
<html>
<body>
Hello World!
    <script>

    </script>
</body>
</html>
```

The page contains no elements inside the head or body of the page, only a "Hello World!" message. When the page is loaded, a tree of these elements is created that allows the page head and body to be controlled.

SET A DYNAMIC TITLE

Use the following code in your script block to set the title for your page:

```
var date = new Date();
var year = date.getFullYear();
document.title = "its " + year;
```

We are using the **Date** method and **getFullYear** to dynamically retrieve the current year in JavaScript. We then set it on the page with **document.title**, which lets us take control of the page to insert our content. This means the year on the page will always stay up to date.

Add this additional code underneath to update the page content:

```
var newContent = "<h1>The page has been updated!</h1>";
document.body.innerHTML = newContent;
```

Here we use the innerHTML method to replace the body content with our new content. As we are inserting HTML we can create a new <h1> tag on the page. Checking in the browser and in the DOM inspector you will see the new title tag and h1 tag. By updating our web pages we can make them active rather than containing only fixed, static content.

CHANGING ELEMENT VALUES

Alter page values by controlling the page DOM with JavaScript.

We can take control of the page elements, or DOM, in JavaScript to control the appearance and behaviour of our web pages. Using this will enable us to alter or replace existing page content to make pages live and interactive.

We will demonstrate this by building a lottery numbers generator, which will create six numbers when requested and add them to the page. Building this involves attaching our generated content to existing page elements to adjust the content. Begin by adding this code to a blank HTML page:

```
<!doctype html>
<html>
<body>

    <h1>Lottery Numbers</h1>
    <div id="results"></div>

    <button id="getNum">Pick number</button>
    <button id="reset">Reset</button>

<script>

</script>
</body>
</html>
```

This simple page contains an empty <div> tag for adding our lottery numbers to, plus two buttons to generate and reset the numbers.

ATTACHING OUR ELEMENTS

We begin our JavaScript code by attaching our HTML elements to variables using **getElementByID**, creating variables for the buttons to set functions when they are clicked. We also create a variable for the results div so that we can update its contents with the numbers.

```
var button = document.getElementById("getNum");
var results = document.getElementById("results");
var reset = document.getElementById("reset");
```

CREATING THE NUMBERS

Next, we create the function for generating a number. We create an array called "current" to contain our numbers, then use a combination of the **Math.round** and **Math.random** to generate a number between 1 and 50. Our number is pushed into the array then the results div is updated using the **innerHTML** method. Note the additional "if" block that checks the array length, so that it will only generate numbers up to 6.

```
var current = [];
button.onclick = function() {
    var number = Math.round(Math.random() * 50);
    if(current.length < 6) {
        current.push(number);
        results.innerHTML = current;
    }
}
```

This should now pick a random number and populate the page with an additional number (up to 6) each time the button is clicked.

RESETTING

To reset, we create an additional function which simply resets the "current" array, then adjusts the HTML element accordingly.

```
reset.onclick = function() {
    current = [];
    results.innerHTML = current;
}
```

This is a simple example of how specific page elements can be targeted and their contents adjusted where needed. Note that the application is simply replacing the results' div each time with the numbers, which are kept in the memory of the array variable. In the next section we will add to existing content.

CREATING AND APPENDING

Create and add elements to the page in JavaScript by building a helpful to-do list.

In the last section, we updated DOM element values and altered their contents with randomly generated content. We can also receive user input and, rather than replacing an element's contents entirely, append to the existing values.

In this section we will build a helpful to-do list application, which takes user inputs and appends them to a list. Begin with this basic page setup in a new HTML file:

```
<!doctype html>
<html>
<head>
</head>
<body>
    <label>To do</label>
    <input id="item" type="text" />
    <button onclick="addItem()">Add item</button>
    <div>
        <ul id="myList">
        </ul>
    </div>
<script>
</script>
</body>
</html>
```

There are a few new things to note here. Firstly, we have set an input field for our inputs with the type set to "text," which will allow any selection of characters to be entered. Secondly, we have added an onclick attribute to our button so the function **addItem** will be called when clicked, rather than setting up the event handler in our JavaScript script block. Finally, we have created an empty <ul> tag with ID "myList," which will contain our items.

CREATE OUR NEW ITEM

For making our application work, we need first to grab the value entered in our input field. We create the **addItem** function (which is called when the button is clicked) then assign the value of our text field to a variable. Then, we use **createElement** to generate a new HTML <li> tag, and set it's contents to our input value. Add this code in your script block:

```
function addItem() {
    var itemText = document.getElementById("item").value;
    var listItem = document.createElement("li");
    listItem.innerHTML = itemText;
}
```

We now have our new list item, so let's add it to the list on our page.

APPENDING CONTENT

By using the **appendChild** method, we can add our new item as a child of the <ul> element on the page. This will add the item into our list as a new element but not replace the existing content, meaning we can keep adding new items wherever needed. We have also added an additional instruction to reset the value of our input box so users know that their item is added and won't accidentally add it twice. Add this code inside your **addItem** function below the first section:

```
document.getElementById("myList").appendChild(listItem);
    document.getElementById("item").value = "";
```

Save and test this in your browser. You should be able to continually add items to your list application. Being able to generate and add page elements is a great example of how JavaScript can enhance a web page by controlling the DOM. We still can't mark items on the list as "done," and they are reset when you refresh the page, but we will look at these issues in future sections.

CHANGING ELEMENT ATTRIBUTES

Use JavaScript to adjust attributes and settings of HTML elements.

Using JavaScript we are able to not only create elements and alter content, but also set and edit element **attributes**. We saw in the previous chapter that HTML elements can sometimes contain attributes to add additional definition, such as the <style> tag for adding inline CSS, or an "href" to add a link destination in an <a> tag. In the same way that we have accessed and changed the text content of elements, we can use various methods to change HTML attributes, giving us more control over web pages.

CHANGING AN IMAGE

As an example of changing an element attribute, you can swap an image on your page by changing the image's src attribute (see page 107). Using .src and providing a new image path will swap out your image. Try this code (you will need to add the two images for the demo to work):

```
<!doctype html>
<html>
<body>
<img id="theImg" src="sunny.jpg">
<button onclick="changeImg()">Change</button>
<script>
function changeImg() {
    document.getElementById("theImg").src = "rainy.jpg";
}
</script>
</body>
</html>
```

CHANGING AN ELEMENT STYLE

A common requirement is to make **style** adjustments to page elements, such as to highlight or notify users of elements on the page, or even to make things appear or hide. In this example, we will make a series of buttons, which when clicked will change the color of an <h1> tag. Begin with the HTML code:

```
<h1 id="heading">Click buttons to change my color!</h1>

<button onclick="changeClr('red')">Go red</button>
<button onclick="changeClr('blue')">Go blue</button>
<button onclick="changeClr('green')">Go green</button>
```

We will be calling a **changeClr** function, with a color argument passed in. The JavaScript function then uses the **.style** method to set the color to the parameter provided:

```
<script>
function changeClr(clr) {
    document.getElementById("heading").style.color = clr;
}
</script>
```

There are various methods available to selectively edit page elements, which can be searched online as required. The important thing to grasp from this exercise is the value and potential in being able to edit HTML elements and their attributes. Other things you could change include:

- Setting the page title

- Switching an external stylesheet to change the page appearance

- Setting the page loaded in an **iframe**

- Disabling a form field to prevent input

SAVING INFORMATION

Learn to save your information using the browser local storage API.

We may sometimes want to keep information from our applications, as when the page is reloaded, so too is the code and all the variable values. In a more advanced application, data would be saved into a database which could then be retrieved and loaded onto your page, but for now we will work with browser storage.

Browser storage is a tool you can use in JavaScript to save information values into your browser. They can then be retrieved and used in your page or deleted. There are two types of browser storage **API**: session storage, which will last as long as your browser tab, and **local** storage, which will last until you close your browser entirely. These storage types are not very permanent but will allow some basic data storage.

To set a **token** in JavaScript, you use the `.setItem` method with two values: the name of your **storage key** and the information you want to store:

```
localStorage.setItem("myData", "Hello");
```

We can then retrieve the "Hello" message using the `.getItem` method, which requires only the value of the key you wish to retrieve:

```
localStorage.getItem("myData");
```

REWORKING OUR TO-DO LIST

On pages 170–171, we created a to-do list app that can take user input and append it to the page. We will now revisit the script to save the values. After building the working list, clear all the JavaScript and add this code:

```
function addItem() {
    var itemText = document.getElementById("item").value;
    listItems.push(itemText);
    localStorage.setItem("todos", JSON.stringify
```

```
    (listItems));
    populateList();
    document.getElementById("item").value = "";
}
```

Here we have adjusted our **addItem** method, which instead of adding a list item to the page directly adds the value to an array and stores the array as a **localStorage** item called "todos." We are using a **JSON.stringify** method here to store the items as an array list. After we call a **populateList** method, which is defined with this code:

```
function populateList() {
document.getElementById("myList").innerHTML = "";
for (var i = 0; i < listItems.length; i++) {
    var listItem = document.createElement("li");
    listItem.innerHTML = listItems[i];
    document.getElementById("myList").appendChild(listItem);
};
}
```

The **populateList** method resets the list on our page and re-populates it using a for-loop of items in our **listItems** array. We have added the code to add items and populate the page, but we also want to retrieve items already added so they can be added to the list:

```
var savedList = JSON.parse(localStorage.getItem("todos"));

if(savedList) {
    listItems = savedList;
    populateList();
}
else {
    var listItems = [];
}
```

Here we use the **.getItem** method to retrieve our saved to-do list items. If there is saved previously added data it will then run the **populateList** method to build the page, otherwise it will create an empty array for new items to be added.

Browser storage is more typically used for temporary information, like a user login session, or items in a shopping basket, but can be a valuable asset in building smart applications as the information doesn't require extra loading to save and retrieve.

JQUERY

Speed up your code with the jQuery JavaScript library.

In our previous chapter looking at HTML and CSS, we saw that external libraries can enhance your projects by supplying additional tools. JavaScript libraries can also enhance and simplify your JavaScript coding, and one of the most common JavaScript libraries that is used in may popular websites is **jQuery**.

jQuery is written in JavaScript, but creates a series of shorthand tools and methods that enable you to access DOM elements and perform tasks with much greater simplicity than using plain (sometimes called vanilla) JavaScript. In this section, we will learn how to attach jQuery then use it to create some simple tasks.

ADDING JQUERY TO YOUR PROJECT

To add jQuery to a project, first visit jquery.com, then click the download button to get the latest version. Download the compressed JavaScript (.js) file then add it to your project folder. You will then need to reference it in your page with a <script> tag in your HTML file.

```
<script src="jquery-3.1.1.min.js" ></script>
```

SIMPLIFYING JAVASCRIPT

Using jQuery, you can massively reduce the amount of code you write. For example, to reference the <a> tags in your page, your would need to use this code:

```
document.getElementsByTagName("a")
```

With jQuery, you can do the same with this code:

```
$("a")
```

Or to make an element hide when a button is clicked you'd need this code:

```
document.getElementById("button").onclick = function() {
  document.getElementById("item").style.display = "none";
}
```

Whereas in jQuery it would be this:

```
$("button").click(function(){
$("#item").hide();
});
```

In jQuery, you reference DOM items using the dollar symbol ($) rather than long **declarations**, and there are many quick readable functions like hide, show, append, and HTML which are quick and logically named.

JQUERY VS JAVASCRIPT

Considering that it uses much simpler syntax and is much quicker, you may be wondering why we didn't begin by learning jQuery, or why we even learned standard JavaScript at all? This is a debated subject as it is true that new learners may find it much easier to get to grips with jQuery and start building with greater ease. Ultimately, though, jQuery is still JavaScript and commonly used tools like variables, loops, and functions remain the same, so you may
find it more logical to learn the core skills first. You may also find scenarios in which it is quicker to use plain JavaScript and the jQuery library requires an unnecessary extra amount of loading.

Some learn jQuery first then use their understanding to grasp plain JavaScript, while others will do so in reverse. To be successful coding JavaScript you will probably need a decent understanding of both, so find a way of learning that suits you.

ADJUSTING ELEMENTS IN JQUERY

Learn some basic jQuery functions to quickly adjust page elements.

In the last section we introduced the jQuery library and how it can enable quicker coding in JavaScript. We will now look at a simple jQuery function in some more detail and revisit our to-do list application, which we built on pages 170–171 and added browser storage to on pages 174–175.

ANALYZING A JQUERY FUNCTION

jQuery is still basically JavaScript, but with some boosted support to help you. Look at this function for example, which will add a class to an element when a button is clicked:

```
$(".button").click(function() {
    $("#element").addClass("new-class");
});
```

- The dollar sign targets the HTML element with the class **.button**. Like in CSS, we target classes with a dot and ID with a hashtag.

- The **.click()** function is a jQuery function adapted from the JavaScript onclick method. Anything inside the following parentheses will happen when the element is clicked.

- Inside the function, we target a new element with ID "#element" then use the jQuery function **.addClass** to add a new CSS class to that element. The class added—"new-class"—follows in parentheses.

This function could be adapted in many ways to achieve different results. For example, changing **.click** to **.hover** will mean the function is carried out when the element is hovered. Changing **.addClass** to **.removeClass** would remove the specified class to change styling, or changing the targeted element inside the function to **$(this)** would apply the change to the element clicked itself.

ADJUSTING OUR TO-DO APP

Revisit our to-do app one last time, now add a style block to the <head> tag in the top of the page with a new class for completed items :

```
<head>
    <style>
    .done {
        text-decoration: line-through;
    }
    </style>
</head>
```

Now attach jQuery to your project (details on pages 176-177). Be sure to add the jQuery reference above your existing script block so the page will understand your new code. We will add a new jQuery function to toggle our **.done** class for list items when they are clicked: add this code inside the **populateList** function:

```
$("li").click(function(){
    $(this).toggleClass("done");
});
```

Now try clicking your list items, they should show a strikethrough display. Click them again and they will return to their original view. You can add any additional styling to make this page look a little clearer and the "done" items more distinct.

USING (THIS)

In this example, we used **$(this)** rather than referring to a specific element on the page. In JavaScript, "this" can be used to refer to the item invoking the function, which is helpful in an instance like ours in which we only want to target one specific "li" element. Be careful as the target of (this) will change based on the structure of your function and where it is referred to.

JAVASCRIPT PROJECT 3: CREATE A QUIZ

Test your friends with a mini quiz using jQuery.

We have covered an introduction to JavaScript and introduced some core coding concepts, and now it's time to explore and learn through building your own projects. In this section we will give a walk-through suggestion for how you might build a quiz application, but with plenty of room to style and develop it further.

BUILDING THE QUIZ

Begin with the basic HTML page outline, plus a <p> tag with your question and a <div> tag containing your options and a submit button.

```
<!DOCTYPE html>
<html>
<body>
<p>Which programming language is this page build using?</p>
<div>
    <label><input type="radio" name="q1" value="1"> Ruby</label>
    <label><input type="radio" name="q1" value="2">Python</label>
    <label><input type="radio" name="q1" value="3">Javascript</label>
    <label><input type="radio" name="q1" value="4">PHP</label>
    <label><input type="radio" name="q1" value="5">.NET</label>
</div>
    <button id="submit">submit</button>

<script src="jquery-3.1.1.min.js"></script>
<script>
</script>
</body>
</html>
```

We are using radio buttons, which are form elements that allow only one to be selected at one time. Each radio input must have the same name attribute and a value for what that selection equals. We have used numbers for each answer value.

CHECKING THE RESPONSES

Now for the script. Inside the second (empty) <script> tag in your page, add this code for when the button is clicked:

```
$("#submit").click(function(){
    var answer =
$("input[name=q1]:checked").val();
});
```

This will create a variable for the answer by finding the value of the checked radio button. Note we are using the shorthand `.val()` jQuery function. Inside the same function we want to check the variable and return a response to the user based on their answer:

```
if(answer == 3) {
    alert("correct!");
}
else {
    alert("wrong, try again!");
}
```

You have a working quiz!

IMPROVING THE PROJECT

You could add more questions by duplicating the body HTML for the question and radio boxes. Be sure to change the radio boxes' name field for each question. Rather than alerting the response you could create a "score" variable and increment based on the cumulative answers given. Then, after analyzing all the questions you could alert to tell the user their score and how well they did. Or, rather than an alert, you could populate your feedback onto the page itself!

JAVASCRIPT PROJECT 4: BUILD AN IMAGE GALLERY

Discover how to build a simple image gallery in jQuery.

In this final project example we will introduce a few other areas for discovery by building the beginnings of an image gallery with jQuery. Image galleries can be a great way to enhance a static web page, and building one can be done in many different ways. Create a folder for this project and add a collection of images you want to use, then create a new HTML file containing our setup code:

```
<!DOCTYPE html>
<html>
<head>
<style>
img {
    width:200px;
    height: 200px;
}
</style>
</head>
<body>

<img id="image" src="#" />
<button id="next">Next</button>

<script src="jquery-3.1.1.min.js"></script>
<script>
</script>
</body>
</html>
```

We have included some basic styling to make our images the same size, then an <img> tag with no image src defined. We have a button for the next image and our jQuery defined in the bottom of the document.

DEFINE YOUR IMAGES

Writing in your empty script block, create an array of your image names, and make a variable of the currently selected image (starting with 0):

```
var images = ["coffee.jpg","rocket.jpg","cat.jpg","cake.jpg"];
var current = 0;
```

Next, create a **changeNum** function, which will use jQuery to set the src attribute value of our image, selecting the index from our "images" array based on the **(num)** parameter passed into the function. Call it immediately, setting the image to our "current" index of 0:

```
function changeImg(num) {
    $("#image").attr("src", images[num]);
}
changeImg(current);
```

Finally, hook up the "next" button to increment the current variable then call the **changeImg** function again. We have an additional check that if the current variable exceeds the number of images it will reset to 0, meaning the gallery will continue to loop:

```
$("#next").click(function(){
    if(current == images.length - 1) {
        current = 0;
    }
    else {
        current++;
    }
    changeImg(current);
});
```

IMPROVING THE GALLERY

As well as a "next" button you could add a "previous" button to view the prior image, it will also need to check the "current" variable does not go below 0. You could also create a list of captions, and enable users to click on them to view a particular image. You could also use jQuery to hide the "next" button when the "current" variable reaches the last image, or hide the previous button when viewing the first image.

CREATE YOUR OWN JAVASCRIPT PROJECT

Take some inspiration and try building your own project.

As with the chapters on Scratch and HTML, beyond our introductions there is still much to learn and explore in JavaScript. It can take a while to gain confidence in understanding and writing JavaScript, especially when facing the frustration of a project not working as expected. You will probably need to revisit sections of this book after attempting your own coding, but the best way to motivate yourself is by finding exciting projects to build. Here are some more areas to explore and ideas for projects to attempt.

CREATE AN ANIMATION STAGE

Mimic the animation effects of Scratch by creating some custom animations in JavaScript. Create a custom animation in CSS and assign it to a class. Then, using jQuery add this class to an element using the **addClass()** function. This could be used alternatively to play music, show and hide page elements, and make all kinds of interactive content.

CREATE A TIMER USING DELAY()

Using the jQuery **.delay()** function, you can make the page wait for a specific amount of time. This could be used to create a countdown timer for a specific day or time that will unveil some information, or an alarm notification page. You could make a helpful timer and find interesting ways to display the time, or build a stopwatch app that will record times on a stop/start button.

CREATE YOUR OWN CALCULATOR

We have seen that JavaScript is great for simple mathematical functions, meaning you could easily build your own calculator application. Start by building the interface with buttons the user can click to create sums, then add your own features where users can save sums and results, round up decimals or output multiplications.

BUILD A SECRET MESSAGE ENCODER/TRANSLATOR

Create an **algorithm** that converts each alphabet letter into the one after (A becomes B, B becomes C etc.), meaning you can add a message and see it scrambled. Then, add an alternate feature in which users can enter their scrambled message and see it converted back into the readable text. Save it and share with friends for your own secret message encoder.

REVISIT OUR PROJECTS WITH IMPROVEMENTS

Remember each of the projects we built as examples in this chapter could be developed with new features. Some have suggestions at the end of how they could be improved, or apply features from one example to another (such as using local storage to save lottery numbers).

SUMMARY

What we have learned in the JavaScript chapter.

In completing the JavaScript chapter, we have reached the end of a linear progression of grasping coding ideas and principles. We began general concepts, practiced these in Scratch, then enhanced them with some intricate development of HTML pages in JavaScript. It can take a long time to fully engage with the concepts presented in these chapters, but in doing so you will give yourself a strong understanding of what coding is and how it is applied. If you have completed the tasks in this chapter and have begun to build your own mini-projects, you may benefit from learning a different programming language to see the similarities and differences, or by taking on more involved projects and development environments. These are topics we will address in the final chapter.

REMEMBER

- JavaScript is a programming language used to give HTML web pages interactivity and behavior.

- Named functions carry our requested tasks when called, can take parameter values and end with a return value.

- By referencing DOM elements, you can create, edit, and delete any page elements or change their values and attributes.

- Using the browser storage API, you can save values that will persist even after the page is refreshed.

- The jQuery JavaScript library allows easier coding and simpler functionality and is ideal for many JavaScript tasks.

5 TIPS FOR YOUR CODING PROJECTS

(1) **Add comments:** In JavaScript, as with most languages, there is an easy way to add comments to help describe and maintain your code. Adding two forward slashes (//) to the beginning of a line will not include that line in the interpreted code. Adding comments helps you keep track of functions and variables, and will help you remember what your code does.

(2) **Consider names carefully:** You can name your variables anything, but you should consider the naming carefully. Calling a variable "myVar" will not mean anything and could become confusing. Calling it something descriptive will help others understand your code, and should help you plan out your projects.

(3) **Avoid duplication:** Variables need to be unique. Using the same name twice may overwrite one. It is better to write long names such as "myTotalBasketAmount" than "total" to avoid duplicating.

(4) **Be realistic:** When planning projects, there is often a tendency to dream up cool but overambitious projects. It's good to be excited about what you could create, but starting too large can lead to disappointment and frustration. A good idea may be to plan out how you would intend to make something—if there are too many unknowns, it may make sense to start with a scaled down project and gradually improve it.

(5) **Ask for help:** In Scratch it was possible to learn by viewing other user's projects. With JavaScript there are many online repositories and examples of code for you to look up and copy. Even experienced coders will find themselves searching online for help with problems or the correct syntax, so don't be shy about searching help online.

FURTHER LEARNING

Keep on learning and teaching yourself and your kids with these great online tools.

This book has focussed on introducing ideas through explanation, demonstration, and an emphasis on creative exploration, but there are various other methods that you may find helpful. Using some great online tools, you can learn from interactive software and courses and create and share your code to improve your understanding. The world of web development is fast-moving, with new languages and frameworks constantly emerging and upgrading, so it's worth keeping an eye on the latest trends in the industry.

CODE STORAGE

As mentioned in the last section, some languages require an involved setup before you can begin sampling and learning on your own computer. Rather than getting bogged down in installations, use online tools that let you quickly get coding.

Trinket

Trinket (https://trinket.io) is a code repository site that lets you build samples for your coding projects easily. Rather than saving files to your computer as we did in previous chapters, create files online to build HTML pages and try out coding in Python.

Codepen

CodePen (codepen.io) is another online tool for storing and sharing code. Its simple interface updates visually as you code, and lets you quickly add external libraries (such as jQuery) with a few clicks. Save "pens" to your account, then share them with others and browse other people's projects for ideas.

GitHub

Github (https://github.com/) is slightly more advanced code repository, as it involves "pushing" your code to an online space from your computer's command-line interface. This site is used by many developers to control versions of their files and collaborate with others. It is also a great place to find and download cool code examples to build upon.

LEARNING TOOLS

Code School

Code school (https://www.codeschool.com/) is a fun and accessible site for learning code through videos and mini challenges. It is free to sign up and has courses in HTML, JavaScript, Ruby, Python, and many others, each with a fun theme to make it more entertaining. Complete courses to gain badges for your online profile, plus some helpful suggestions for further learning.

Codecademy

Codecademy (codecademy.com) is another online learning platform with more focus on coding exercises. Complete mini tasks to progress through courses in different languages and libraries. Gain detailed feedback on how the code works and what it does and try to keep your coding "streak" running as long as possible.

Code Avengers

Code Avengers (www.codeavengers.com) is a paid service with a free trial. It lets you learn languages by playing interactive coding challenges, but has a specific focus on building particular projects.

Free Code Camp

Free Code Camp is a (www.freecodecamp.com) non-profit self-teaching site where you can learn by building real world projects.

Khan Academy

Khan Academy (www.khanacademy.org) is a free online community for learning many skills including coding languages.

OTHER LANGUAGES

Explore alternative coding languages to develop your understanding and improve your skills.

Following the chapters in this book will not only introduce you to what coding is and how it works, but will give you some experience with the creative and varied types of problem solving that can be achieved through its use. We have also seen that many coding principles are shared from **Scratch** to **HTML** to **JavaScript**, with a difference in what each language is used for and how it is written.

There are many different types of programming language, each with different structures and **syntax**, but also with different key benefits and flaws. Choosing which languages to learn will depend on what they will allow you to build, and you may also find that some feel more logical and intuitive to pick up. Learning additional languages is highly recommended, as it will enhance your understanding and coding skills. It is also much easier to learn new languages after learning the first one, as the similarities will become clear and you will not be starting completely from scratch. Here are some examples of other languages to investigate.

```
def myfunc(
msg ):
    print msg
    Return
```

PYTHON

```
def combine_
value(a,b)
    a + b
End
C-Head Php
```

RUBY

```
<?php
function writeHello() {
    echo "Hello world!";
}
writeHello();
?>
```

PHP

WHAT'S THE DIFFERENCE?

Python is a simple and easy-to-learn programming language similar to JavaScript, and is also used for building websites and games. Python is also used on compact programmable devices such as Raspberry Pi, and is a popular choice for learning to code. Its syntax is remarkably simple—look at this function example:

```
def myfunc( msg ):          }    function name & parameter
    print msg               }    print
    Return                  }    return statement
```

Ruby is also a modern language used to build websites. It is used in the popular "Ruby on Rails" (RoR) framework to build large database applications. Here is an example function in Ruby:

```
def combine_value(a,b)
    a + b
end
```

PHP is a language used in many websites as part of the Wordpress blogging platform, and is also the language running Facebook. It is very popular and easy to set up. Here is an example function:

```
<?php
function writeHello() {
    echo "Hello world!";
}
writeHello();
?>
```

SETTING UP

Unlike JavaScript, you will not be able to simply run and test these languages straight from HTML files in your browser. Most development languages will need you to download them and run a local server, so a quicker way to start learning would be through online tools and courses. We will look at some options in the next section.

ADVANCED TOPICS

Looking ahead, if you continue learning and practicing your coding skills, there are amazing feats you can accomplish, and projects you can build.

Once your code knowledge has grown in fluency, and you have a good understanding of the basics, you may wish to go further by exploring some advanced topics. Complex programming is beyond the scope of this introductory book, but take a look here for a few suggestions for ambitious new topics to research. Looking ahead can also be inspirational for you and for your kids, when you are feeling frustrated with learning the building blocks of coding.

APPLICATION DEVELOPMENT

By setting up a development framework on your computer, you can begin to build software, applications, and games with advanced features like databases, user accounts, dynamic routing, and content. There are many excellent guides and walk-throughs to building web applications online, which can enable you to take your coding to the next level.

APIs

An **API** (application programming interface) is a set of functions for any application or the tools to use something. Using public APIs, anyone can access these tools to get information from another website—an example would be using the Twitter API to load your tweets into a web page, or the YouTube API to load some video search results. There are also many tutorials and courses on APIs and how to access them in projects, which can enhance websites by leveraging the popular features of others.

WEARABLES

If you want to get your coding projects out in the physical world, there are now many fantastic opportunities with mini-computers. Small, cheap devices such as the Raspberry PI, Arduino, or BBC Micro:bit are programmable machines that allow you to take advantage of their size and built in tools to create many interactive creations. Track real environmental events like movement, lights, directions, temperatures, speed, location, or time to make them light up, display information, or even trigger moving elements—there are endless possibilities. Different machines are programmed in different coding languages, but some can even integrate with Scratch. The devices are largely geared towards new learners and are worth exploring if you are motivated by physical hardware integrations.

FINAL TIPS

You've reached the end! Here are some final suggestions to help guide your coding path.

Hopefully this book will help you to understand coding and encourage you to take your knowledge further. Writing code and developing projects can be a fun but challenging task, so here are some helpful strategies for maintaining a steady progression.

Be creative

As you may have found in our mini-projects, there is more than one way to achieve something. Solving coding challenges requires creative thinking to find the most efficient and effective way of processing information, which is part of what makes coding fun. Development can involve some dry technical learning, so finding new ways to learn and create project ideas will give you more motivation to keep going when it gets tough.

Stay adaptive

We have also discussed how there are many different coding languages and types of coding purpose, which are changing all the time. An effective coder will not just have a keen eye on learning from other people's code, but also an ear to new trends and emerging tech in the industry. There are always fast-moving ideas about to which languages and frameworks are the best to learn, so becoming stubborn about changing from what you know could ultimately lead to you being stuck in outdated coding habits. While it's good to take time and learn, and perhaps even develop preferred languages and setup, it pays to be adaptive to what could be coming next

Learn in stages

The world of coding can seem daunting and complicated when starting out—even some of the examples in this book would seem baffling to new starters. Like most new things, it's good to pace yourself and take your time grasping new concepts. When learning how something works, try to experiment—see what doesn't work, try variations, and become comfortable before moving onto something more complicated. The aim should always be to gradually gain confidence and make new challenges familiar, rather than get swamped in confusing intricacy too quickly.

Be persistent

Coding can be fun, but it's not always! As you progress, you will likely come across things that seem nonsensical, inexplicably do not work, or just have a constant feeling of being blocked by new problems. Don't give up—there is commonly a honeymoon period starting out, then a tough phase of independent progression before the eventual climb to confident coding—you just need the persistence to push through a tricky patch. When finding things frustrating, stay motivated by moving onto something else for a while, revisiting learning material, or even searching for help from others. Dedicated concentration and persistence in improving your knowledge will see you rewarded with coding experience.

Be inspired

Remember, there are many fantastic resources for learning, but absolutely anything could serve to inspire you. See an impressive feature on a website? Learn how it was done or devise a way to replicate it yourself. Thought of a common everyday problem? Devise an app to solve it. Once you have some of the coding theory in place the world is yours to build and create as you see fit, and staying inspired will keep you coding happy.

GLOSSARY

These key terms are bolded throughout this book, and are worth learning and remembering.

Alert
A sound or message that indicates some predefined event has occurred or a selected operation is about to be performed.

Algorithm
An algorithm is a set of instructions designed to perform a specific task.

and/or
An and/or statement is used in conditional instructions to apply when multiple combinations of conditions are met, as opposed to and if/else, statement, which only applies when a condition is either true or false.

API
Stands for "application programming interface." An API is a set of commands, functions, protocols, and objects that programmers can use to create software or interact with an external system. It provides developers with standard commands for performing common operations so they do not have to write the code from scratch.

Arguments
A parameter or "argument" is a value that is passed into a function. Most modern programming languages allow functions to have multiple parameters.

Array
An array is a list of pieces of information. These can be text, numbers, or variables, and enable code to iterate instructions to every item in a list. Arrays are a helpful tool for storing groups of information and records.

Attribute (HTML)
An attribute is an additional setting added to an HTML tag. Examples include the href attribute on a link to define its link location or the style attribute to set an element's visual settings.

Body
The body element contains all the contents of an HTML document,

such as text, hyperlinks, images, tables, and lists.

Boolean

Boolean, or Boolean logic, is a subset of algebra used for creating true/false statements. Boolean expressions use the operators AND, OR, XOR, and NOT to compare values and return a true or false result.

Bootstrap

Bootstrap is a commonly used CSS framework that enables web designers to quickly build web pages using pre-built elements.

Browser

Browsers are computer programs with a graphical user interface for displaying HTML files, used to navigate the Internet. Examples include Google Chrome, Safari, etc.

Bug

A bug is an error in a software program. It may cause a program to unexpectedly quit or behave in an unintended manner.

CDN

A CDN or Content Delivery Network is a file hosted remotely for you to reference when creating your web pages. An example would be the jQuery library, which can be copied and saved locally, or accessed directly. Using a CDN can make your site load faster and is easier to set up, to avoid having to manually code all elements.

Camel case

The practice of writing compound words or phrases so that each word or abbreviation in the middle of the phrase begins with a capital letter, with no spaces or hyphens (camelCase). This is commonly used in JavaScript.

Class

In HTML, any tag can have a class applied to it. This enables the tag to be identified with JavaScript or for unique styling to be applied with CSS. A class is referenced in CSS with a prefixed dot (.element).

Computational thinking

The structured, logical thought process behind coding is referred to as computational thinking, because it essentially means you are learning to think like a computer.

Conditional

A conditional statement is a set of rules performed if a certain condition is met. **Conditional flow** refers to a whole function, or process, which involves multiple opportunities for decision-making, but continues on in all eventualities.

Config

A config or configuration is a setting you define in order to avoid replication and to make programming easier. For example, if you are coding a game, you may set a car speed to a number variable, meaning you can then refer to it to make the car move.

Console

A console is the combination of a monitor and keyboard. It is a rudimentary interface in which the monitor provides the output and the keyboard is used for input.

CSS

CSS stands for "Cascading Style Sheet." It is used to format the layout of web pages. They can be used to define text styles, table sizes, and other aspects of web pages that previously could only be defined in a page's HTML.

Debugging

Debugging means eliminating as many errors from a programme as possible. This debugging process often takes a long time, as fixing some errors may introduce others.

Declaration (CSS)

A declaration applies a visual change by combining a property and a value, separated by a colon (such as color: blue). A **declaration block** can contain multiple declarations, separated by semicolons. Multiple declarations in a block are called **chained declarations**.

Developer tools

Developer tools are built in to modern browsers to let you view and analyze your code.

DIV tag (HTML)

A container unit that holds the different elements of a page and divides the HTML into sections.

DOM

Short for Document Object Model, the specification for how objects in a web page (text, images, headers, links, etc.) are represented. The DOM defines what attributes are associated with each object, and how the objects and attributes can be manipulated.

DRY

Stands for "don't repeat yourself." A principle of software development aimed at reducing repetition of all kinds of information.

Dynamic

Refers to actions that take place at the moment they are needed rather than in advance.

EMS

Ems are a measurement used in CSS for spacing and font size. Unlike using pixels, which are fixed numbers, ems use percentages so give you a relative sizing system.

Error

An error is a term used to describe

any issue that arises unexpectedly and cause a computer to not function properly. Computers can encounter either software errors or hardware errors.

Events

In programming, an event is an action that occurs as a result of the user or another source, such as a mouse being clicked or a key being pressed.

File type

Images come in varied formats, such as gif, jpeg, and png. These are examples of file type. You can usually see the filetype defined in the file name or in the file properties.

Flow

Flow refers to the steps of the algorithm being completed in their designated order

Formatting (CSS)

Formatting is a style applied to elements with various CSS properties. These enable your HTML text elements to appear in italics, bold, different size and colors, or even underlined or crossed out. This book also discusses formatting code, meaning structuring it properly.

For-loop

A for-loop defines a list of variables, then can be used to run a defined code on each variable on the list. For-loops are made up of four statements: initialization, conditional, iteration, and loop body (the code to be executed).

FTP

Stands for "File Transfer Protocol." FTP is the most common way of sending and receiving large files between two computers.

Function

A function is a group of instructions, also known as a named procedure, used by programming languages to return a single result or a set of results.

Gotcha

A valid construct in a system, program, or programming language that works as documented, but is counter-intuitive and almost invites mistakes because it is both easy to invoke and unexpected or unreasonable in its outcome.

Hardware

Computer hardware refers to the physical parts of a computer and related devices. Internal hardware devices include motherboards, hard drives, and RAM. External hardware includes monitors, keyboards, mice, printers, and scanners.

Head

In HTML, the head is the first section in the code that contains information about a web page's properties and links to external related files. It is denoted by a pair of opening and closing <head> tags.

HTML

Stands for "hypertext markup language." HTML is used to create electronic documents (called pages) that are displayed on the World Wide Web. Each page contains a series of connections to other pages called hyperlinks. Every web page you see on the Internet is written using one version of HTML code or another.

ID (HTML)

Elements in HTML can have an ID setting applied to them, which gives them a unique identification. Generally each element should use a different ID, which can then be targeted by CSS or JavaScript to alter the element. IDs are usually defined with a hashtag (#myElement)..

if/else

An if/else statement in programming is a conditional statement that runs a different set of statements depending on whether an expression is true or false.

iframe

When writing in HTML, the <iframe> tag is a block element used to designate an inline frame, which allows the user to embed an HTML document into the current web page.

Indentation

The process of adding small indents to your code in order to improve the display and legibility.

Index

In lists (or arrays), each item has an index, referring to its order in the list. In coding lists often use zero-indexing, so the index of the first item is 0. Indexes can also be used in for loops to refer to the item being analysed in each loop.

Input

Whenever you enter data into your computer, it is referred to as input. This can be text typed in a word processing document, keywords entered in a search engine's search box, or data entered into a spreadsheet. Input can be something as simple as moving the mouse or clicking the mouse button or it can be as complex as scanning a document or downloading photos from a digital camera.

Instruction blocks (Scratch)

These blocks are color-coded puzzle-piece shapes that are used to create code in Scratch. The blocks connect to each other like a jigsaw puzzle, where each data type (event, command, reported value, reported boolean, or script end) has its own shape and a specially shaped slot for it to be inserted into — this prevents syntax errors. Series of connected blocks are called scripts.

Integer

An integer is a whole number (not a fraction) that can be positive, negative, or zero. Therefore, the numbers 10, 0, -25, and 5,148 are all integers. Integers cannot have decimal places.

JavaScript

JavaScript is a programming language commonly used in web development. It was originally developed by Netscape as a means of adding dynamic and interactive elements to websites.

JPEG

Short for Joint Photographic Experts Group, this is a raster image graphics compression format. JPEG is abbreviated as .jpg in the file extension used with IBM compatible computers.

jQuery

jQuery is a JavaScript library that allows web developers to add extra functionality to their websites. It is open source and provided for free under the MIT license. In recent years, jQuery has become the most popular JavaScript library used in web development.

Key frame (CSS)

Keyframes are animation frames, and in CSS keyframes are a type of animation that left you define individual display properties at different stages of the animation.

KISS

An acronym for Keep It Simple, Stupid. This is a general term used in many contexts but in coding is particularly relevant to simplifying when planning and implementing any functionality.

Link

A link is a word, address, image or button that can be clicked and will take you through to another document. In HTML, a link can be added to a web page using <a> tags (anchors).

List

A list is a type of variable, also called an array.

Local

In networks, local refers to files, devices, and other resources at your workstation. Resources located at other nodes on the networks are remote.

Loop

In computer science, a loop is a programming structure that repeats a sequence of instructions until a specific condition is met. Programmers use loops to cycle through values, add sums of numbers, repeat functions, etc.

Markup language

A markup language is a computer language that uses tags to define elements within a document. It is human-readable, meaning markup files contain standard words, rather than typical programming syntax. While several markup languages exist, the two most popular are HTML and XML.

Media query

Media queries are a feature of CSS that enable web page content to adapt to different screen sizes and resolutions. They are a fundamental part of responsive web design and are used to customize the appearance of websites for multiple devices.

Minified

When code is reduced to it's simplest form, it has been minified.

Modal

A modal is a window that forces the user to interact with it before they can return to their page.

NaN

Stands for "not a number." In mathematics and computer programming NaN is an undefined or unrepresentable value, especially in floating-point calculations. For example, 0/0 or the square root of a negative number would return a NaN result.

Nested function

A function that runs inside of another function.

Output

Data generated by a computer is referred to as output. This includes data produced at a software level, such as the result of a calculation, or at a physical level, such as a printed document.

Parameter

In computer programming, a parameter or "argument" is a value that is included in a function. Most modern programming languages allow functions to have multiple parameters.

Pixels

Stands for "picture element." These small little dots are what make up the images on computer displays, whether they are flat-screen (LCD) or tube (CRT) monitors. The screen is divided up into a matrix of thousands or even millions of pixels. Typically, you cannot see the individual pixels, because they are so small. This is a good thing, because most people prefer to look at smooth, clear images rather than blocky, "pixelated" ones.

PHP

Stands for "Hypertext Preprocessor." PHP is an HTML-embedded web-scripting language. This means PHP code can be inserted into the HTML of a web page.

Property (CSS)

In CSS, settings are applied with a combination of the property and the value. For instance, in setting the color to red, color would be the property while red would be the value

Pseudo element (HTML)

In HTML, a pseudo element means a subsection of an element, which is usually used for targeting in CSS. Examples include the hover state of an element or settings for before and after an element.

Python

Python is a high-level programming language designed to be easy to read and simple to implement. It is open source, which means it is free to use, even for commercial applications.

Refactoring

Improving the design of existing software code. Refactoring doesn't change the observable behavior of the software; it improves its internal structure.

Remote

In networks, remote refers to files, devices, and other resources that are not connected directly to your workstation. Resources at your workstation are considered local.

Responsive

A responsive program is one which can react to user input, interacting with the user.

Return (JavaScript)

A return is a term used in JavaScript to declare the end result of a function. If you want your function to conclude your can use return and pass back any result as the conclusion of your function.

Ruby

Ruby is an object-oriented programming language.

Semantic Tag

In HTML5 new tags were introduced to make HTML more logical and easy to read. Rather than building a page with many ambiguous Div tags you can now use semantic tags like Head, Section, Article and Footer.

Scratch

Scratch is a programming language that makes it easy to create interactive stories, animations, games, music, and art.

Script

A script or scripting language is a computer language with a series of commands within a file that is capable of being executed without being compiled. In Scratch, a script is the name for a series of connected instruction blocks.

Software

Software is a collection of instructions that enable the user to interact with a computer, its hardware, or perform tasks. Without software, computers would be useless

Sprite (Scratch)

A sprite in Scratch is any element added to the stage which can be animated or adjusted with script instructions.

String

A string is a data type used in programming, such as an integer and floating point unit, but is used to represent text rather than numbers. It is comprised of a set of characters that can also contain spaces and numbers.

Style (CSS)

The style attribute is used for adding inline CSS to an HTML tag.

Style block (CSS)

CSS styles can be inline (using the style attribute, as above), or they can be added in blocks, which can contain multiple style settings. Style blocks are applied to elements throughout a page, rather than just one specific element, as is the case with inline styling..

Syntax

Syntax is a set of rules for grammar and spelling. In other words, it means using character structures that a computer can interpret.

Tag

When referring to HTML, XML, or other markup languages, a tag is an element inserted into a document or file that changes the look of content or performs an action. An HTML element has an opening tag that contains the name and any attributes and a closing tag that contains a forward slash and the name of the tag being closed.

Text Editor (HTML)

A text editor is a computer program for editing text. Although the HTML markup of a web page can be written with any text editor, specialized HTML editors can be useful as they will automatically organize code to make it easier to read..

This

This is a programming term used in languages like JavaScript to refer to the item invoking a function. For example, then applying a function on any list item being clicked "this" would refer to the specific list item.

Token (JavaScript)

In JavaScripts, a token is a keyword, variable name, number, function name, or some other entity in which you should never insert a space or line break.

Type

Each variable has a type which restricts which methods can be applied to it. Examples include strings, integers, Booleans and lists.

User

An individual who uses a computer. This includes expert programmers as well as novices.

Variable

In programming, a structure that holds data and is uniquely named by the programmer. It holds the data assigned to it until a new value is assigned or the program is finished. Common types of variable include integer, Boolean, string, and list.

Web font

On a web page, an HTML font or web font is the type of text displayed, designated using CSS.

Zero indexing

Zero-based numbering or indexing is a way of numbering in which the initial element of a sequence is assigned the index 0, rather than the index 1 as is typical in everyday non-mathematical/non-programming circumstances.

INDEX

ACKNOWLEDGMENTS

Frazer Wilson is a web designer and developer based in London. He would like to acknowledge Anna Wilson Cox, Mark Batup, John O'Dwyer, and Michael Hartl for their support and guidance.

Weldon Owen would like to thank Frazer Wilson, Dr. Camille McCue, Samuel Murray, and Lucy Kingett for their indispensable help with this project; and also the talented artists of Shutterstock.com for their contributions.

Weldon Owen take great pride in doing our best to get the facts right, but occasionally something slips past our checks. Therefore we welcome corrections and wherever possible, will endeavor to incorporate them into future editions of this book.

Disclaimer

Kids—before getting online, please ask your parents. Parents, be mindful that the Internet is a public space and you should supervise and/or educate kids appropriately.